CREATIVE SPEECH – THE NATU

CREATIVE SPEECH

THE NATURE OF SPEECH FORMATION

Aphoristic records of courses
on the cultivation of Speech as an Art

Essays and notes from seminars and lectures

Rudolf Steiner
Marie Steiner-von Sivers

Translated by
Winifred Budgett, Nancy Hummel, Maisie Jones

RUDOLF STEINER PRESS
LONDON

Rudolf Steiner Press
51 Queen Caroline Street
London W6 9QL

First English edition 1978
Reprinted 1999

Originally published in German under the title *Methodik und Wesen der Sprachgestaltung* (volume 280 in the *Rudolf Steiner Gesamtausgabe* or Collected Works) by Rudolf Steiner Verlag, Dornach. This authorized translation is published by kind permission of the Rudolf Steiner Nachlassverwaltung, Dornach

Translation © Rudolf Steiner Press 1978

A catalogue record for this book is available from the British Library

ISBN 1 85584 087 1

Cover design by Andrew Morgan, incorporating artwork by John Baker
Printed and bound in Great Britain by Cromwell Press Limited, Trowbridge, Wiltshire

TRANSLATORS' NOTE

This is an attempt to convey the content of *Methodik und Wesen der Sprachgestaltung* in the English language, and we are very much aware of its shortcomings. We hope nonetheless that it will serve to awaken interest in the Art of Speech Formation.

The reader is asked to remember that everything said and written referred originally to the German language.

The English equivalents of the exercises are those made by Maisie Jones and used in the London School of Speech Formation. Others are also in use elsewhere, notably those made by Alice Crowther, Maud Surrey, Hans Pusch, Mechthild Harkness, and Sophia Walsh.

CONTENTS

8

II

INTRODUCTION

In the year 1923 Rudolf Steiner was asked to write his autobiography. In the weekly publication *Das Goetheanum* he began a series of articles, *The Story of my Life*, which were suddenly disrupted in the spring of 1925 by his death on 30 March. A short time before, in order to characterize his path of development in which his opponents thought they saw contradictions, he had described the spiritual situation at the turn of the century and recalled what had moved him at that time. It is revealing to see to which sphere of life Rudolf Steiner in retrospect refers.

In the twenty-ninth chapter of his autobiography he says: 'In the realm of the spirit new light on the evolution of humanity sought to break through into the knowledge acquired during the last third of the nineteenth century. But the spiritual sleep in which this acquired knowledge was given its materialistic interpretation prevented even a notion of the new light, much less any proper attention to it.

'So that time arrived which ought by its own nature to have evolved in the direction of the spirit, but which belied its own being, the time wherein it began to be impossible for life to make itself real.

'I wish to quote from articles I wrote in March 1898 for the *Dramaturgische Blätter*, which had become a supplement of the *Magazin für Literatur* at the beginning of 1898. Referring to the art of lecturing I said: "In this field more than in any other the learner is left wholly to himself and to chance. . . . Because of the form which our public life has assumed almost everybody nowadays frequently has need to speak in public. . . . the elevation of ordinary speech to a work of art is a rarity. . . . We

11

lack almost wholly the feeling for the beauty of speech, and still more for speech which has style. . . . No one lacking knowledge of correct singing would have the right to discuss a singer. . . . In the case of dramatic art the requirements are far less. Fewer and fewer people know whether or not a verse is properly spoken. . . . Nowadays they often look upon artistic speaking as ineffective idealism. . . . We could never have come to this had we been more aware of the ability to cultivate speech artistically. . . ."

'What I then had in mind could come to a form of realization only much later within the Anthroposophical Society. Marie von Sivers (Marie Steiner), an enthusiast for the art of speech, was the first to dedicate herself to a genuinely artistic form of speaking. With her help it then became possible through courses in speech and drama to work towards the raising of speech to a true art.

'I venture to introduce this subject here to show how certain ideals have sought their fulfilment throughout my life, although many people have tried to find contradictions in my development.'

And the following words are almost the last which Rudolf Steiner wrote in his autobiography: 'An artistic performance was included in the programme of the Congress in Munich in 1907. Marie von Sivers had long since translated Schuré's reconstruction of the Eleusinian drama. I edited the text for a dramatic performance. This play was then included in the programme. So a link was created with the ancient Mysteries, even if only in a tenuous form. But the important thing was that the Congress had an artistic element, an element ensuring that the spiritual life within the Society should not in future be bereft of art. Marie von Sivers, who played the role of Demeter, pointed the way even in this presentation to the nuances which drama was to acquire within the Society. . . .'

We can follow this development from the first review of a performance in the Vienna Burgtheater (1889) up to the last lecture course *Speech and Drama*,* held in Dornach in September

* Anthroposophical Publishing Company, London, 1960.

1924. What Rudolf Steiner had already said at the beginning of our century concerning the art of speaking as an impulse emanating from speech itself has been available in book form for years in *Veröffentlichungen aus dem literarischen Frühwerk.** Soon after his death Marie Steiner made the content of the *Speech and Drama Course* available to the public. The bibliography at the end of this book shows the huge amount of work done by Rudolf Steiner in this sphere. A great loss is the absence of a work to which Marie Steiner referred in 1926 in her preface to the *Speech and Drama Course*. She said: 'This book will soon be followed by another which must provide the groundwork for that which has been given in these lectures. It will give practical instruction, speech exercises, and a method of working through which one can most directly reach the goal – the mastery of speech formation and style. It will consist mainly, but in a somewhat condensed form, of what I gave in some practical sessions prior to these lectures. The participants of the course made an attempt at the speech exercises which had been given to us by Rudolf Steiner with explanations and instructions on previous occasions and many a speech course which I had to hold was thus given new life. They form together with this book a coherent whole, and in this way give a complete picture of what can take the place of physiological, mechanical methods in order to free the brimming life-forces of speech and to raise them to the level of art.'

Essential as this book would have been, in the course of a quarter of a century's unswerving work in the service of the Anthroposophical Movement it was never written. A book for which the pupils of Marie Steiner and many others had waited for years was therefore irretrievably lost. In the course of the years Marie Steiner tried again and again to give form to the promised work. She even started writing the text, or tried to find ways of expressing certain essential viewpoints, as we can see from some of the work now published. But the pressure of work and the excessive demands made upon her did not allow her time to finish the book. The texts published here can in no way

* Sektion für redende und musische Künste, Goetheanum, Dornach, 1936.

take its place. Imagine what would have come about had Marie Steiner been able to write this book out of the wealth of her experience – she who had a fluent command of German, Russian, French, English and Italian, and was thus in a position to penetrate into the very depths of the poetry of the different peoples!

Through the greatness of her art and of her teaching something often arose simply through one word, through one remark in a rehearsal, which bore fruit for many of her students long after the immediate moment had passed, which had the effect of 'enkindling life, bestowing life, pouring itself into our very being'. Just before her death Marie Steiner was working on plans for this text-book and entrusted the carrying out of this task to some of her pupils. She was particularly anxious to publish the speech exercises which Rudolf Steiner had given. And so, in bringing out this book, we honour a pledge.

There is above all widespread interest in these exercises and Rudolf Steiner's explanations of them, even though they are often used without naming the author or referring to him. The speech exercises found in Rudolf Steiner's posthumous works were almost without exception in his own handwriting, but in some cases in an unfamiliar version, and these we now include. The text conforms to the original manuscript. It is surprising how these exercises came into being as a direct response to a demand arising from life itself in the year 1919, which was an incisive point of time within the Anthroposophical Movement. We cannot go here into the development of speech formation through Marie Steiner in the first two decades of this century, but would draw attention to the book *Aus dem Wirken von Marie Steiner** which contains an outline of her life. At the end of the First World War people surged into the Anthroposophical Society from every direction. In Dornach stood the Goetheanum. Rudolf Steiner planned the performance of the four Mystery Plays for the summer of 1923. At that time it was primarily the young people who carried the impulse to make Anthroposophy fruitful in the world. The movement for the

* Dornach, 1951.

Threefold Social Order had arisen. Rudolf Steiner gave with open hands in all directions.

At this time the following occurred: 'It must have been in May of the year 1919', writes Emil Leinhas,* 'that the demands made on my voice by the many lectures and talks given during workers' meetings made me realize that my voice was not correctly placed. I therefore asked Rudolf Steiner whether he could not advise me and my colleagues within the working group of the Threefold Social Order as to how our voices could hold out better. Rudolf Steiner agreed immediately and said he would ask Frau Dr. Steiner to give us some exercises. A few days later Emil Molt, Dr. Carl Unger, Hans Kühn and I met Rudolf Steiner and Frau Marie Steiner in the red room of the Anthroposophical Society, Landhausstrasse 70, Stuttgart, and received from them the first speech exercises. After this Rudolf Steiner attended these lessons several times. These exercises were made partly to meet our individual needs, and I remember that Rudolf Steiner gave the exercise *Erfüllung geht* . . . especially for Emil Molt, who was somewhat short of breath.' This then was the beginning of the instruction which has been used for decades in the training in speech formation. A chronological table at the end of this book lists the most important dates in connection with this work.

From the beginning of her work it was Marie Steiner's wont to record, or at least make notes of all Rudolf Steiner's lectures and instructions, and as a result many notebooks exist which are of the greatest value for us today. We also possess a series of notes for the speech courses she had to give, during which Rudolf Steiner usually added explanations. These notes constitute an essential part of this book. She would often make more than one fair copy of them. It is true they are not without gaps, yet in spite of this, and bearing in mind their direct personal contact during that time, we possess a great amount of really comprehensive working material. This we have decided to publish in spite of its aphoristic character. To be sure, the reader must be prepared to find the same exercise more than once in different places or in a

* See also Emil Leinhas, *Aus der Arbeit mit Rudolf Steiner*, Basel, 1950.

different context, but just because of this he may perhaps find his way into the essential nature of practice, which rests on the continual repetition of the familiar. These entries are especially valuable because of the occasional remarks added by Rudolf Steiner in his own hand. We have not put these notes together in a pedantic fashion, but as they organically arose. They relate primarily to the courses held in the summer and autumn of 1922, which correspond almost word for word with each other. Furthermore, all Marie Steiner's work on the nature of speech formation which was found posthumously has been included in this book.

Instructive remarks with which Marie Steiner had in all probability wanted to commence her text-book, and which for that reason we have put at the beginning, serve as introduction to that section dealing with method. A seminar for teachers of speech formation was held in Dornach in the winter of 1927, and the references were found in a notebook of that time. It was then that Marie Steiner compiled the fundamental work *Die Kunst der Rezitation und Deklamation*,* from transcripts of lectures given by Rudolf Steiner. Practical examples were worked through with the various teachers, and these form an essential part of the instruction in the seminar. The notes for the first basic speech exercises are still extant, with an accompanying introduction aimed at creating awareness of the true nature of speech formation.

A further attempt was made by working through the notes of the courses held in the summer and autumn of 1922. Without this wealth of material we should be dependent on transcripts neither revised nor corrected by Rudolf Steiner or Marie Steiner. These are still scattered around as unauthorized notes.

A combination of various circumstances led to these courses on speech. In the first place it was neither actors nor prospective reciters who sought stimulus for their training, but primarily friends from the Youth Movement who, as we said before, strove to realize Anthroposophy in a practical way. The artistic field offered possibilities on every hand. The following interesting

* Rudolf Steiner Nachlassverwaltung, Dornach, 1967.

remark was made by a course participant: 'It was said at that time that a performance of the Mystery Plays was being planned at the Goetheanum; that suitable people had to be found and that with this in mind a preparatory course was to be taken by Dr. and Frau Dr. Steiner.' In these courses the speech exercises given in 1919 were repeated, after which Rudolf Steiner gave new exercises, thus extending in various ways the sense for the sounds of speech. This resulted in a right style of speech for lyric and epic poetry and the distinction was made between recitation and declamation. The foundation was laid for the next step into the dramatic and this has a special background. Georg Kugelmann, who at that time had just taken over the Directorship of the Neukünstlerische Bühnenspiele in Rostock, was present with his wife at this course and he wrote to Rudolf Steiner asking many important questions concerning the production of medieval miracle plays with students and young theatre enthusiasts. We see yet again how Rudolf Steiner responded to the circumstances of life by giving helpful practical instructions. Thus there arose the first instructions concerning 'speech formation for the stage', as he designated it. They also studied some dramatic scenes and the corrections which Rudolf Steiner gave at that time seem to us to be of such value that we are printing these also in the appropriate place.

It is surprising therefore that the wealth of instruction for style in speech, which underwent further development in Holland in 1923, was not given in the first place to those interested professionally as was the case, for example, with the courses for doctors and scientists. It was not until the autumn of 1924 that the *Speech and Drama Course* was held. This also had 'a little history', as Rudolf Steiner remarked at the time. This time it was professional stage artists working in various ways who brought this course about. Approximately eight hundred people took part, so great was the interest in the art of the theatre. Soon after it was announced it became clear that it would not be possible to limit the number of participants as originally planned. 'It might perhaps have acquired a different character' wrote Marie Steiner, 'but in this way it acquired a

17

broad human trait.' So from the outset, speech formation was placed within this all-embracing human framework.

It was then to those engaged in the educational movement that Rudolf Steiner urgently recommended the cultivation of the art of speech. We have the speech exercises given in 1919, which were published in the course of the years in connection with the educational work, and which are also included in the first part of this book. In the course of the seminar, educational problems claimed more and more time so that Rudolf Steiner was able to give only a few examples of recitation, but these were really appropriate. In the second part of the book indications may be found which Rudolf Steiner gave within the conferences held by the teachers of the Waldorf School in connection with speech formation and the teaching of the German language. These remarks are of the greatest value in spite of their aphoristic character, and if they are consistently nurtured as germinal beginnings they can produce the most beautiful results. Even here everything arose from life, evoked through situations arising in various classes or through the questions of the teachers themselves.

Another important field is the training of lecturers in the art of speaking. At the beginning we pointed out how the speech exercises came into being through lecturers recognizing the need for the training of their voices. Even at the beginning of the century Rudolf Steiner had written of the urgent necessity of a school teaching the art of lecturing. The instructions which Rudolf Steiner gave to speakers in 1921 in the orientation course *Anthroposophie, Soziale Dreigliederung und Redekunst* (Rudolf Steiner Verlag, Dornach, 1971) were a continuation of those given previously and relevant parts of these lectures are published here.

Only a few exercises in speech formation for therapeutic use are available, though doubtless if Rudolf Steiner had been granted more time he would have given a great many more. A hitherto unpublished indication concerning speech disturbances may be found in a conversation about Spiritual Science which took place during the first High School Course at the

18

Goetheanum in 1920, and which is now published in *Eurythmie, die Offenbarung der sprechenden Seele* (Rudolf Steiner Verlag, Dornach, 1972). These verbal indications show on what delicate observation this sphere of speech formation depends. What Rudolf Steiner said in his lecture of 13 October 1923* concerning the healing forces lying within the breath is already well known.

The aphoristic remarks which Rudolf Steiner had written for the members of the General Anthroposophical Society during the *Speech and Drama Course* (Anthroposophical Publishing Company, London, 1960) form the final cadence of this book. Once again the path is described, indicating how shape and form can be given from out of the forces of speech.

May the present age bring to this most human of all spheres of life the necessary understanding. To Rudolf Steiner and Marie Steiner, who restored to the art of speech its Mystery character and human quality, this understanding would be the truest expression of gratitude.

Dornach, Whitsun 1955   Edwin Froböse

---

* *The Four Seasons and the Archangels* (Rudolf Steiner Press, London, 1968).

> In order to encompass with thought the
> essentialities of the spirit and give them shape and
> form in ideation one needs mobility in the activity
> of thinking. It is acquired by imbuing the soul
> with the artistic element.
>
> RUDOLF STEINER

Experiencing the Word leads to intimacies in spiritual cognition that have the effect of unveiling mysteries concealed in man. Man confronts us here in accordance with his innermost being from out the very foundations of the life that has created him, as he has been formed by the direction-giving forces of the moving stars – the planets, and of the fixed stars – the zodiac, that have in the sounds their signs, in the signs their seals. If we grasp their comprehensive sounding within the language given to man by the gods, then we experience new states of consciousness. These states of consciousness wrest us from the torpor of excessive intellectualization and bring us closer to the source of existence. If we immerse ourselves in the sounds we also free our thought from encapsulation in the grey matter of the brain which sucks the life out of it having become, instead of the pliant and supple instrument it should remain, a vampire, killing thought. If we bring thought back again into the speech that gave it birth, into its sounds, its lights and shades, its colours and pictures, into the beating of its pulse, the rising and falling of its sounds, its tendencies to movement, its depths, breadths and heights, its zones, its plastic, resilient, contracting and dispersing forces – then indeed we experience worlds that are the richer and lovelier the more we are in a position to separate them from our subjective feeling, and enter into the life of the whole universe. How poor we appear with our narrow life of feeling in comparison with the wealth we acquire by entering into the objective life of the universe. Speech shows us ways of doing this. In it we touch on the divine forces which have made us and which are our masters and guides. We touch on creative powers that have made for themselves an instrument in man.

MARIE STEINER

I

RUDOLF STEINER

BASIC CONDITIONS FOR
ANTHROPOSOPHICAL ACTIVITY

Great difficulties arise because the real impelling force of the Anthroposophical Movement is not sufficiently appreciated everywhere in the right way. Here and there we still hear judgments expressed which are a pure denial of the Anthroposophical Movement inasmuch as they draw parallels between it and that which it should supersede in the course of human evolution. It occurred again a few days ago that someone said to me: 'If we place what Anthroposophy has to give before one person or another, even the most matter-of-fact and practical will accept it, but we must not mention Anthroposophy or Threefold Social Order to them; these we must deny!' This is something many people have done for many years. It is the worst thing we can do. We, as representatives of anthroposophical life, must take our stand everywhere in the world under the sign of the whole truth in whatsoever sphere it may be, and we must be aware that if we cannot do this we are unable to be of any real service to the Anthroposophical Movement. Ultimately no good can possibly come of a veiled representation of the Anthroposophical Movement.

Of course, everything must be taken individually. One cannot make hard and fast rules. I will give some examples, my dear friends, to explain what I mean.

There is eurythmy. Eurythmy, as I said at yesterday's demonstration, is derived from and is being developed out of the deepest foundations of anthroposophical life, and we must be absolutely aware that with eurythmy, imperfect as it may be at

25

present, something absolutely new and original is being placed into the world which can in no way be compared with anything else in the world which may have an apparent similarity. We must arouse such enthusiasm for our cause as to exclude any possibility of external and superficial comparison. I know how easily such a saying may be misunderstood but I nevertheless say it to you here, my dear friends, because it expresses one of the most fundamental conditions under which the Anthroposophical Movement may thrive within the Anthroposophical Society.

Or, to take another example, I have had to sweat much blood recently – figuratively speaking of course – over all the discussions that have taken place concerning the form of recitation and declamation that has been evolved within our Society by Frau Dr. Steiner. As with eurythmy, the root-nerve of this declamation and recitation is one that has been produced and nurtured from the very depths of Anthroposophy and this we must acknowledge. We must acknowledge this and not believe that something better would emerge if we were to introduce scraps here and there of something which is good, or even better, in other seemingly similar systems. Of this original and primal character we must be fully aware in all spheres of our work.

A third example. One of the domains in which Anthroposophy can become especially fruitful is that of medicine, but you may rest assured that Anthroposophy will remain unfruitful for medical science and for the real art of healing if the tendency continues within the medical work of the Anthroposophical Movement to push Anthroposophy as such into the background, or to present the medical part of our work in such a way as to be pleasing to those who represent medicine from the contemporary point of view. We must have the courage to carry Anthroposophy itself in the narrower sense, with that which eurythmy should be, with that which recitation and declamation should be, with that which medicine should be and with much else that lives within our Anthroposophical Society.

With this I have given you some indication at least of the basic conditions we must have in mind at the beginning of the meeting* for the founding of the General Anthroposophical Society.

* Christmas 1923–24.

MARIE STEINER

PATHS TO THE ARTISTIC
UNITY OF PRIMAL POETRY

Anthroposophy is the basis for understanding what is intended by the new speech formation. It is necessary first and foremost to have anthroposophical insight in order to grasp what would live and grow in this respect. If we are to reach beyond a purely intellectual understanding to a deeper experience of the things with which we are here concerned, we must find the inner approach to the sources of esotericism. This gives us a feeling of being anchored in the whole of the Cosmos. Within this we are as an eye gradually opening to the light in the same way in which the physical eye, at first made corneous through the intensity of the light, is awakened out of dullness through the stimulus of the senses to become a reflector of the light, an organ of the evolving ego.

We had as our goal the production of Rudolf Steiner's Mystery Plays, and to all who learned from them, the obstacles on the path became clear and they undertook the work with selfless patience and devotion. Like a tributary springing from the creative power of the source, choral speaking arose and led deeper into the spirit of its origin. By means of intense concentration, which allowed the power of the ego to direct and rule unchecked within the element of the will, without being deadened by mechanistic intellectualism, it was already possible to obtain good results.

The most difficult task of all is the bringing of real life, carrying power and spiritual fire into the speaking for eurythmy. The demands made here on the speaker are indeed immense.

Selflessness is the prime necessity in creative artistic activity. One must be able to forget oneself.

Eurythmy weaves in the element of spirituality. It makes use of the human body as an instrument through which to express what lies in the formative power of its life-body, in that which Schiller characterizes in *Das Ideal und das Leben* as 'godlike among gods, the form'. The formative force is the basis of the physical body and holds it together. It is a spiritual force. If it leaves the body and hands it over to the forces of nature, the body disintegrates. The forces of lifeless nature disperse it, whereas the forces which create, build and form it are spiritual. They have fashioned man, they have fashioned the world. The world is the Word of the spirit; man is the Word of the world. When he becomes a servant of the Word he must feel those forces through which he has been placed in the Cosmos and allow these forces to hold sway within his spoken word. He must forget himself and bring to expression what lives and weaves within the forces of the Word. These are revealed through gesture in the art of eurythmy. The human body surrenders to them. If the powers of direction, dynamic, balance, carry and thrust live in the spoken word, then the word and the movement inherent in the form flow together in inner and outer gesture. If the speaker burdens the word with his own subjectivity, if the word is a welcome opportunity for releasing the forces of his own passionate nature, if he mirrors himself complacently in the word, draws it into himself and wallows in it instead of learning to flee himself as pure flame or surrendering willingly and with artistic sense to the forces of form, then he has not yet freed himself from the fetters which the age of materialism, with its cult of physical sensuality and the drive for personality, has imposed upon him – then indeed he cannot liberate the cosmic man within himself, and remains imprisoned in the tomb of his own personality. Yet eurythmy is an art so deeply rooted in the spirit that it is necessary even to develop a new inner organism in order to become its instrument. This is especially so if it is to be apprehended in its invisibility, in gesture submersed in word, which now through the instrument of the human body becomes visible on the stage; the word, which through the speaker must be transformed into carrying power, which in turn must become a formative and dynamic force in the body-free stream of air.

The difficulties of this path are so great that many practising artists, striving and struggling in different spheres, have come to the conviction that speech is the most difficult art of all.

So indeed it is, when one realizes that all creative forces are hidden within it, all plastic forces and all sounding forces. These need to come to expression in it, freed from the fetters which chain it to matter.

But how can we achieve this?

It is not enough to be able to mirror the subjective experience of a dramatic figure on the stage. It is important instead not to colour with our own subjectivity a character created by a poet, foreign to us in its whole being, but to free it from ourselves in its objective form. A dramatic figure, however, always contains within it its own subjectivity into which we must transform ourselves.

Epic poetry demands complete objectivity. Space and time, story and character, should all sound, integrated in their essentialities. To this end we ourselves must become transparent.

Lyric poetry of a spiritual nature makes the same demands. We must submerse ourselves in the godhead, we must expand to the divine. We do this only by learning to feel the creation of the Gods, the Cosmos. The creation of the Gods is reflected in the sounds of speech, which form the world sculpturally through the consonants and ensoul it inwardly through the vowels. We should feel the forces of the sounds of speech as the beating of wings which, independently of ourselves, bear us willingly out into the Cosmos. A hard path, for we must free the spirit from the subjective forces of the soul, from the element of feeling as well as from the intellect, and we must allow the archetypes of the consonants, the formative forces, to work within the cosmic sphere of soul. We must bear our own inner being outwards and follow it.

For eurythmy, even lyrics of a personal nature must be spoken in such a way that the inner being is poured outward and not the outer drawn in. If this should happen, the eurythmist in moving with the gesture of the word would need to draw her limbs continually in towards herself, and would be impeded, hampered, in the unfolding of her movement. If inner feeling is transformed into formative force pressing outwards, sculpturally and musically released in the stream of the breath, coloured with tonal quality and imaginatively ensouled, then the inner eurythmy of the word becomes the carrying power of the eurythmist, who has to perform the external gesture and has to free the body from the force of gravity, raising it into the power of etheric movement. The service the speaker renders to eurythmy is received back in twofold measure as a gift, through the key it gives to the artistic element of speech.

'The impulse for speech springs from the astral organization modified by the ego.' The animal is unable to give utterance to speech. The everyday speech of man remains rooted in the unconscious, but speech as an art must raise the unconscious into consciousness.

In olden days speech was felt and experienced as an art. Primal speech was primal poetry and was expressed in rhythm, beat, assonance, alliteration and the measured tread of the syllables. Thought and feeling lived within it as a unity. Now thought has become abstract, feeling has drawn inwards and between them lies speech which has become prosaic. The paths must be found again which lead to this artistic unity of primal poetry. In order to find them again Rudolf Steiner points to the importance of the five Greek gymnastic exercises through which the human being learns to feel his place within the order of the cosmos, to feel his relationship to the earth and to the things of the external world.*

The draft for this article probably stems from the year 1926 or 1927 at the latest, so it arose at the time when the work started with the actors, who in the course of the following years came more and more to Dornach. Most of them had also taken part in the *Speech and Drama Course* in 1924, in which Rudolf Steiner had spoken of the results already mentioned of research into spiritual science and the connection of the five Greek gymnastic exercises with the art of the stage. We refer here to the basic anthroposophical books and in addition to the lecture cycle *The Wisdom of Man, of the Soul and of the Spirit* (Anthroposophic Press, New York, 1971), which is of particular importance for the study of art, especially the first four lectures.

RUDOLF STEINER

SPEECH EXERCISES WITH EXPLANATIONS

RECORDED BY MARIE STEINER FOR A TEXT-BOOK ON SPEECH FORMATION

In giving speech artistic shape and form the healthy co-operation and harmonization of body, soul and spirit becomes manifest. The body shows whether it is able to incorporate the spirit correctly; the soul reveals whether the spirit lives in it truly; and the spirit is vividly present working directly into the physical. Those taking part in speech courses have a direct personal experience of the revelation of Anthroposophy in the activity of man.

Here it may be regarded as a testing of Anthroposophy that it is in a position to enable the art of speech to come to life again, in its full significance, for it has been led into a helpless situation through the materialistic outlook prevailing in the world. Enthusiastic participation in courses given by Marie Steiner on the art of speech proves that the significance of 'being able to speak' is meeting with ever-increasing understanding.

RUDOLF STEINER

Only in learning to hear one can learn to speak. The best training for a beginner is to repeat what has been well spoken. In the good old schools, only imitation was allowed to begin with. It is the only correct method for speaking: repeating and learning to hear. You must first go through this process, then find your own way.

The exercises spoken as examples should be repeated in such a way that you go into the sound; you must enter into every syllable, into every sound. You must feel yourself carried by your voice from word to word. Become quite free in doing it, so that you have the feeling you speak with the air around you and not with your throat. You must feel the vibrating air around you and echo this vibrating.

In this way you will learn to know speech as an organism incorporated into that which is correctly heard. You must hear the sound in the air around you. That is where the resonance lies. The organs of speech only provide the ground for making vibrations. You must become aware of your speech organs and learn to feel the patterns of resonance. All searching for resonance in nose, diaphragm, breast and head leads only to mechanization. Natural speaking must arise by your entering into every syllable and also into the consonantal combinations. Later on when you have learnt to do that quite automatically, you can then stress, for instance, the less important syllables more lightly. Physiological resonances lead to one-sidedness. You can achieve everything if you start off with the sounds; if you modulate the sound. Learn how to study an A (ah) and an O (oh), how to make it plastic by bringing the sound forward. Feel how every consonant becomes plastic only when it is made to move differently depending on its neighbouring vowels.

*

The sounds should be felt, should enter into consciousness. For that purpose we use, to begin with, simple exercises in articulation:

34

*Dass er dir log uns darf es nicht loben**
Dart may these boats through darkening gloaming

Nimm nicht Nonnen in nimmermüde Mühlen
Name neat Norman on nimble moody mules

Rate mir mehrere Rätsel nur richtig
Rattle me more and more rattles now rightly

Redlich ratsam	Rateless ration
Rüstet rühmlich	roosted roomily
Riesig rächend	reason wretched
Ruhig rollend	ruined Roland
Reuige Rosse	royalty roster
Protzig preist	Proxy prized
Bäder brünstig	bather broomstick
Polternd putzig	polka pushing
Bieder bastelnd	beady basket
Puder patzend	prudent pertness
Bergig brüstend	bearskin bristled

If you learn to feel your way into every sound, you will become conscious of your instruments of speech.

*

Illuminating with consciousness – that is what we have to strive for. Entering with consciousness into the instruments of speech does not mean merely feeling them intensely in a physical sense, it means freeing the sounds from the physical by penetrating them with consciousness and laying them into the stream of the breath. Consciousness takes hold of the essential nature of the thing and is carried along by it while the intellect can by-pass it in a very strange way. Intellect reflects, photographs, and thereby so easily acquires a mechanical and abstract character, becoming ever more tenuous.

Nowadays, the world understands the word 'Spirit' as intellect. It does not know that the intellect is only a stage on the

* The speech exercises in this book are printed from Rudolf Steiner's own manuscript for the first time.

way towards the spirit inasmuch as it serves to awaken consciousness. It can turn in two directions: towards the spirit, towards clarification and illumination, or towards perception, towards simple deduction. If it remains at this level it will be ensnared by matter, by automatism; it shuts itself off, loses its connection with 'the beyond', becomes in fact a coffin of thought. Its inner death cuts it off from the spirit.

Grasping the essential nature of speech can lead back to the experiencing of the spirit. Let us feel our way towards it slowly, by starting with the basic elements. This means feeling our way towards the sound and the breath, raising them gradually into the sphere of consciousness.

*

Become aware of your breath by letting it go and following it through as it streams out. You need not be bound by any particular method. The method best suited to your organism will come.

Erfüllung geht	Fulfilling goes
Durch Hoffnung	through hoping
Geht durch Sehnen	goes through longing
Durch Wollen	through willing
Wollen weht	willing flows
Im Webenden	in wavering
Weht im Bebenden	wails in quavering
Webt bebend	waves veiling
Webend bindend	waving breathing
Im Finden	in freedom
Findend windend	freedom winning
Kündend	kindling

We have quite short lines here. Use up your breath completely in every line. Take a fresh breath before each new line. Use this exercise gymnastically as it were in order to regulate your breath. Learn to become flexible with the help of the consonants and combinations of consonants. You achieve this by feeling them within the stream of the breath.

36

In the previous exercises you had to direct your attention to the organs against which the sound struck and in this way you were able to become aware of your instruments of speech and to know them. Now you must become aware of the stream of your breath.

It is very useful to practise the words in reverse order, for example: *Wollen – Nellow*.

Unhindered by the sense, you can draw out the inner qualities of the sounds to the full. Try to go with the wave-like movement of the double l, to trace what it does with the O (oh) and the E (eh). You have to learn from the sound itself what you must do in order to utter the sound. Try to hear with your whole being, to hear what the air does when you speak, as if you were in a globe of air and were watching what was happening in the air around you, when the stream of your own breath pours into it. Admittedly, when another person speaks, the ear vibrates more strongly. Hearing yourself is something akin to feeling the sound, as if you wanted to grasp something in your chest and head that was poured through your ears. You feel the sound only if you keep the movements of your eardrum sensitive, as also the vibrations that sound through the Eustachian tubes, starting from your mouth. You grasp them inwardly at first, but the ear resounds in sympathy. In this way you must accustom yourself to hearing, above all to listening to yourself, and that is in a certain respect a feeling.

You must feel the way in which the r rolls differently from the way in which the l casts waves. You should accustom yourself to feeling the part the air plays. Feel the special nature of fricatives, nasals, trills, plosives and sibilants. When seeking the sound, do not proceed from a physiological adjustment of the organs – it never leads to a natural exercising of the organic functions – but start from hearing, from hearing yourself.

What takes place in diaphragm, chest or head should take place unconsciously. You should not have the feeling at all of using the throat and other organs, but the air. You should accustom yourself to feeling what the air does, for instance, when you make the mm sound, or nn, or ll.

You must learn from the sounds all there is to learn. The breath itself must be brought into play unconsciously when you sense the sound and in sensing, hear.

Now we will do an exercise from which you can learn to understand what it means to enter into the sound and to make it live.

> In den unermesslich weiten Räumen,
> In den endenlosen Zeiten,
> In der Menschenseele Tiefen,
> In der Weltenoffenbarung:
> Suche des grossen Rätsels Lösung.

> In the vast unmeasured world-wide spaces,
> In the endless stream of time,
> In the depths of human soul-life,
> In the world's great revelations:
> Seek the unfolding of life's great mystery.

Let the lines gradually grow in intensity. To begin with, take your own sounds with you so that everything sounds and reverberates together; then experience the air resounding outside you, into which you enter with the stream of your breath; learn to hear it; learn to know it as an entity into which you lay your own weak tone, which grows stronger through it and gradually becomes objective.

In the first four lines there lies an expectation which causes the tone to grow in intensity. It attains fulfilment in the fifth line, which expresses quiet cognition arising out of the will in consciousness.

I. Let yourself fall!

Erfüllung geht	Fulfilling goes
Durch Hoffnung	through hoping
Geht durch Sehnen	goes through longing
Durch Wollen	through willing
Wollen weht	willing flows
Im Webenden	in wavering
Weht im Bebenden	wails in quavering
Webt bebend	waves veiling

Webend bindend waving breathing
Im Finden in freedom
Findend windend freedom winning
Kündend kindling

II. Now direct it!

In den unermesslich weiten Räumen,
In den endenlosen Zeiten,
In der Menschenseele Tiefen,
In der Weltenoffenbarung:
Suche des grossen Rätsels Lösung.

In the vast unmeasured world-wide spaces,
In the endless stream of time,
In the depths of human soul-life,
In the world's great revelations:
Seek the unfolding of life's great mystery.

You must acquire consciousness of your breath. You must acquire consciousness of how you hear the sound from within, not from without. Let it go, freed from intellect, then the sound falls into the stream of the breath and is carried along by it.

The essential consciousness of the sound, having been felt, is carried along as well. You yourself, being in it, hear from within and thereby fathom the tonal qualities in the word. If you remain on the surface, only skimming it with your intellect, then you only hear noises, you do not grasp the ringing quality of life.

The first exercise is well suited for finding yourself while letting yourself fall. There is a difference between a sudden plunge into the element of air, like a dive into water, and the slow steering of a boat, as in the second exercise. To begin with, take the helm as an ego-conscious being and let yourself go, surrendering to the element that bears you. But feel the helm, the ego-force, which forms the barque that bears you, the barque of air, into which the stream of your breath is laid. Feel how it glides rhythmically along on the ripples and billows of the air. If you do this, you release something captive within you.

*

Repetition of the two breath exercises may provide the starting point for a new lesson. A real, practical experiencing of all that has been said should be your goal. Learn to hear. Feel your way, tentatively into hearing. Set your breath free, free from yourself. Make it independent, follow it through.

Now a similar exercise in which the structure is reversed:

Du findest dich selbst:	You find your own self:
Suchend in Weltenfernen,	Seeking in world distances,
Strebend nach Weltenhöhen,	Striving toward world heights,
Kämpfend in Weltentiefen.	Struggling in world depths.

The distances, the heights, the depths should all resound.

In order to achieve this you must take the sounds along with you in the stream of the breath. The sounds and their combinations then regulate the stream of the breath. Enter really deep into the vowels and the combinations of consonants that unite with the substance of the external air and are carried along by the stream of the breath. Let yourself be taken with it. Then say it once merely intellectually and notice the difference.

❋

Now an exercise for phrasing according to the sense:

Nimm mir nicht, was, wenn ich freiwillig dir es reiche, dich beglückt.
Deprive me not of what, when I give it to you freely, pleases you!

We have three clauses here: The main clause *Nimm mir nicht* and *was dich beglückt,* and inserted into this a subsidiary clause *wenn ich freiwillig dir es reiche.* This must be shaped differently in speaking from what has gone before. But with *dich beglückt* you take up the same kind of intonation you dropped with *was.*

❋

Now another exercise in articulation:

Lalle Lieder lieblich	Lulling leader limply
Lipplicher Laffe	liplessly laughing
Lappiger lumpiger	loppety lumpety
Laichiger Lurch	lackety lout

Imagine you have a green frog before you with an open mouth and you speak to it with humour and affection. . . . Express the challenge that lies in the words; then you transpose yourself simultaneously into the situation.

*

Exercises purely for articulation, in order to make the organs of speech supple, should be learnt by heart so that you can deal with them really gymnastically. Only when you know them by heart can you reel them off to full advantage.

Pfiffig pfeifen	Piffling fifer
Pfäffische Pferde	prefacing feather
Pflegend Pflüge	phlegma fluting
Pferchend Pfirsiche	fairground piercing

Pfiffig pfeifen aus Näpfen
Pfäffische Pferde schlüpfend
Pflegend Pflüge hüpfend
Pferchend Pfirsiche knüpfend

Kopfpfiffig pfeifen aus Näpfen
Napfpfäffische Pferde schlüpfend
Wipfend pflegend Pflüge hüpfend
Tipfend pferchend Pfirsiche knüpfend

Ketzer petzten jetzt kläglich	Curtsey Betsy jets cleric
Letztlich leicht skeptisch	lastly light sceptic
Ketzerkrächzer petzten jetzt kläglich	Curtsey cressets Betsy jets cleric
Letztlich plötzlich leicht skeptisch	lastly plotless light sceptic
Schlinge Schlange geschwinde	Slinging slanging a swindler
Gewundene Fundewecken weg	the wounding fooled a victor vexed
Gewundene Fundewecken	The wounding fooled a swindler
Geschwinde schlinge Schlange weg	slinging slanging vexed

41

Zuwider zwingen zwar	Tu-whit twinkle 'twas
Zweizweckige Zwacker zu wenig	twice twigged tweaker
Zwanzig Zwerge	to twenty twangy twirlings
Die sehnige Krebse	the zinnia crisper
Sicher suchend schmausen	zither zooming shambles
Dass schmatzende Schmachter	this smartened smacking
Schmiegsam schnellstens	smuggler sneezing
Schnurrig schnalzen	snoring snatching

For making the organs of speech flexible:

Nur renn nimmer reuig	Narrow wren mirror royal
Gierig grinsend	gearing grizzled
Knoten knipsend	noting nippers
Pfänder knüpfend	fender coughing
Klipp plapp plick glick	Clip plop pluck cluck
Klingt Klapperrichtig	clinked clapper richly
Knatternd trappend	knotted trappings
Rossegetrippel	rosily tripled
(1st version:	
Rossegetrampel)	
Marsch schmachtender	March smarten ten
Klappriger Racker	clap rigging rockets
Krackle plappernd linkisch	crackling plopping lynxes
Flink von vorne fort	fling from forward forth
Krackle plappernd linkisch	Crackling plopping lynxes
Flink von vorne fort	fling from forward forth
Marsch schmachtender	march smarten ten
Klappriger Racker	clap rigging rockets

*

For stammerers:

Nimm mir nimmer
Was sich wässerig
Mit Teilen mitteilt

Nimmer nimm mir
Wässerige Wickel
Was sich schlecht mitteilt
Mit Teilen deiner Rede

During the course of these exercises speech defects or disturbing habits that impede an artistic way of speaking usually come to light. Here you have to take things individually of course. Only certain examples can be given. There are, for instance, pinched voices that have to be made more expansive. In this case the following exercise would help:

Ei ist weisslich	Eye is viceless,
weisslich ist Ei	viceless is eye
Blei ist neu im Streu,	Blithe is noise in Troy,
neu im Streu ist Blei	noise in Troy is blithe
Die Maid ist bläulich,	The night is 'broidered,
bläulich maidlich	'broidered nightly

First version: *Ei ist weiss, weiss ist Ei*
Blei ist neu, neu ist Blei
Maid ist bläulich, bläulich Maid ist.

You must watch the difference there between *ei – Blei*, which lies more in the mouth and *ai – Maid*, which lies further back in the throat.

If the tone is trapped in the nose a good exercise to release it would be:

Der Base Nase ass Mehl	The parcel master asks mail
Rasen Masse kratze kahl	rather marshall crafty Carl

Take care that the nasal resonance does not sound as well.

*

Speak with the breath. The breath must not be withheld, but must be a flowing stream. Usually the breath is withheld. Ordinary speaking chops up the stream of the breath. You must overcome this in order to seek that level of speaking in which you become aware of the continuous stream of the breath. It ought to pass through the whole flow of speech like a wind. The words should not stand there like single trees, but the sound should be as of a wind that goes through the trees.

Try to differentiate within the stream of speech itself while swimming in it. For instance:

Sturm-Wort rumort um Tor und Turm
Molch-Wurm bohrt durch Tor und Turm
Dumm tobt Wurm-Molch durch Tor und Turm

Storm wolf roars forth through door and tomb
Bold wolves bored through door and tomb
Doom taught wolves bold through door and tomb

In the first line you can swim in the stream of speech. Now try to feel the difference in the second line; and then again in the third, how that is quite different.

*

Sende aufwärts	Send thou upwards
Sehnend Verlangen	yearning desire
Sende vorwärts	Send thou forwards
Bedachtes Streben	conscious striving
Sende rückwärts	Send thou backwards
Gewissenhaft Bedenken	conscientious reflection

Pay attention here to the shading and nuance of the three lines. Each line requires a certain nuance.

If you want to prepare yourself for something you can start with an exercise such as that above.

Everything depends on the upward, forward and backward progression.

Although the upward line seems to be stronger than the forward and backward ones, a gradual intensification is indicated rhetorically.

Try to sense here how through all six lines the tongue has to become a kind of boat or canoe.

The voice becomes well placed when it is brought into the right position.*

---

* The notes break off here.

RUDOLF STEINER

PEDAGOGICAL COURSE 1919

SPEECH EXERCISES WITH EXPLANATIONS

SOME EXAMPLES OF RECITATION

One must be acutely conscious of the fact that the power of speech is a specifically human property. He must also bring to consciousness the way in which he faces the other three realms of nature. Once he is aware of that, he realizes that language is of central importance in the determining of his ego. . . . Belief that the genius of language works in the organization of language is of great importance. . . . In finding one's way consciously into the structure of language one learns a great deal from the genius of language itself. And learning to feel something concrete about the working and weaving of the spirit of language is of exceptional importance. It is precisely to language that we owe so much in our ego-feeling, in our feeling of ourselves as personality. And in man the feeling can be raised almost to something akin to an attitude of prayer: 'I hear people speaking in the speech round about me, and then the power of language flows into me!'

RUDOLF STEINER

*Rudolf Steiner:** It is really of the greatest importance that we nurture clear speaking, along with everthing else. It has a certain influence, a certain effect. On another occasion† exercises were formulated by me that were constructed less from the point of view of meaning than for the purpose of bringing the organs of speech into motion in an organic way, into an all-round movement. Now I would like you to pass these exercises around without embarrassment and everyone in turn should speak them, so that by practising them often we make our speech organs resilient, make them do gymnastics as it were. Frau Dr. Steiner will speak them first, in an artistic and correct manner, and I would ask the individual participants to repeat them after her. These exercises are constructed not from the point of view of sense or meaning, but for the purpose of exercising the speech organs:

> *Dass er dir log uns darf es nicht loben*
> Dart may these boats through darkening gloaming
>
> *Nimm nicht Nonnen in nimmermüde Mühlen*
> Name neat Norman on nimble moody mules

The m returns again and again, but in a different combination and so the speech organs are exercised in the right way. Dwell longer on the n in *Nimm*; long I (ee), short I (ee); then two n's come together.

> *Rate mir mehrere Rätsel nur richtig*
> Rattle me more and more rattles now rightly

And so the organs come into proper gymnastic activity.

I would advise you to pay special attention to entering literally into the sounds, literally growing into them. Be attentive to this distinct growing into them, so that you are aware that you speak every sound and raise every sound into

---

* Printed from manuscript. Records and notes not revised by the lecturer.
† See Editor's Introduction and also Emil Leinhas: *Aus der Arbeit mit Rudolf Steiner* (Basel 1950, p. 69).

46

consciousness. Skipping over sounds is a very prevalent fault, but speech is there to be understood, and to begin with one should rather stress syllables which are not normally stressed, making a certain caricature of them. Actors practise saying 'friend*ship*' and not '*friend*ship'. Speak every sound consciously! It would even be good if you did such things, albeit not regularly, as Demosthenes who, as you know, in desperation put pebbles on his tongue and through exercising in this way so strengthened his voice that it could be heard above the rushing sound of the water. He did this to improve his delivery so that he could be heard by the Athenians.

*

We will begin with a repetition of yesterday's speech exercises and then take new ones.

Redlich ratsam	Rateless ration
Rüstet rühmlich	roosted roomily
Riesig rächend	reason wretched
Ruhig rollend	ruined Roland
Reuige Rosse	royalty roster
Protzig preist	Proxy prized
Bäder brünstig	bather broomstick
Polternd putzig	polka pushing
Bieder bastelnd	beady basket
Puder patzend	prudent pertness
Bergig brüstend	bearskin bristled

Reading of a fable by Lessing.

Rudolf Steiner: with something of this sort the title need not be specially stressed.

Die Nachtigall und der Pfau

Eine gesellige Nachtigall fand unter den Sängern des Waldes Neider die Menge, aber keinen Freund. 'Vielleicht finde ich ihn unter einer anderen Gattung', dachte sie und flog vertraulich zu dem Pfau herab. 'Schöner Pfau, ich bewundere dich!' 'Ich dich auch, liebliche Nachtigall.' 'So lass uns Freunde sein', sprach die Nachtigall weiter. 'Wir werden uns nicht

beneiden dürfen, du bist dem **Auge** *so angenehm, wie ich dem* **Ohr**.*' Die Nachtigall und der Pfau wurden Freunde.*
Kneller und Pope waren bessere Freunde als Pope und Addison.

The Nightingale and the Peacock

A friendly nightingale found amongst the singers of the wood enviers galore, but no friend. 'Perhaps I shall find one among a different species', she thought, and flew down trustfully to the peacock. 'Beautiful peacock, I admire you very much'. 'I you too, dear nightingale.' 'Then let us be friends,' the nightingale continued, *'we* ought not to be envious of each other. You are as pleasing to the *eye* as I am to the *ear*.' The nightingale and the peacock became friends.

Kneller and Pope were better friends than Pope and Addison.

Dr. Steiner said jokingly: France and Italy are better friends than Italy and England. That may also be said. This can be applied in the most diverse ways.

*

Rudolf Steiner: Today we will try out an exercise which is intended to lengthen the breath.

Erfüllung geht	Fulfilling goes
Durch Hoffnung	through hoping
Geht durch Sehnen	goes through longing
Durch Wollen	through willing
Wollen weht	willing flows
Im Webenden	in wavering
Weht im Bebenden	wails in quavering
Webt bebend	waves veiling
Webend bindend	waving breathing
Im Finden	in freedom
Findend windend	freedom winning
Kündend	kindling

You will only achieve the desired end by dividing the lines up properly. Then the breath becomes rhythmic in the correct way. This exercise is connected with a kind of vocal athletics for regulating the breath.

48

In words such as *Erfüllung* and *Wollen* both l's must be spoken. Do not let an h slip in with the first l but say both l's alongside each other. Try also not to speak with a vibrato, but to acquire a steady tone in the voice which is produced from a deeper point in the chest, enabling one to speak full-toned vowels. The breath should consciously regulate itself before each of these separate lines. The words standing together must be read as belonging together.

In the ordinary way one does such speech exercises as the following:

> *Barbara sass stracks am Abhang*
>
> or: *Barbara sass nah am Abhang*
>
> or: *Abraham a Sancta Klara kam an**.

Reading of a Fable by Lessing.

Das Ross und der Stier

Auf einem feurigen Rosse flog stoltz ein dreister Knabe daher. Da rief ein wilder Stier dem Rosse zu: 'Schande! Von einem Knaben liess ich mich nicht regieren!' 'Aber ich,' versetzte das Ross, 'denn was für Ehre könnte es mir bringen, einen Knaben abzuwerfen?'

---

* The exercise: *Barbara sass nah am Abhang,*
Sprach gar sangbar – zaghaft langsam;
Mannhaft kam alsdann am Waldrand
Abraham a Sancta Clara!

belongs to the material given by the famous teacher Julius Hey in *Die Kunst der Sprache* ('Der kleine Hey'), B. Schott's Söhne, Mainz-Leipzig 1914. Dr. Steiner found these sound-sequences could be used and also mentioned the exercise for E (eh).

> *Es streben der Seele Gebete*
> *Den helfenden Engeln entgegen;*
> *Entdeckend des Herzens Wehe,*
> *Wenn Schmerzen es brennend verzehren!*

We print these exercises in full because they have a certain meaning, while the exercises given by Rudolf Steiner stem purely from the element of sound.

The Steed and the Bull

An impudent boy came flying along on a fiery steed. A wild bull called out to the horse: 'Shame on you! I would not be governed by a lad!' 'But I would', replied the horse, 'for what kind of honour would it bring me to throw the boy off?'

Rudolf Steiner (after all those taking part in the course had read the fable): You will probably feel, now that you have heard it so often, that it is written in the way that fables and many other things were written in the eighteenth century. One has the feeling that they are not quite finished, as many things were not quite finished in those days. Dr. Steiner read the fable through again and then said: Now, in the twentieth century, one would go on with the fable in some such way as the following:

A bull's honour! If I sought honour by obstinately standing still, that would not be a horse's honour, but an ass's honour.

That is how it would be done nowadays. Then children would notice straight away that there are three kinds of honour: a bull's honour, a horse's honour and an ass's honour. The bull throws off; the horse calmly goes on carrying the boy because it is noble; the ass stays obstinately still, because he sees his honour therein.

*

Speech Exercise:

In den unermesslich weiten Räumen,
In den endenlosen Zeiten,
In der Menschenseele Tiefen,
In der Weltenoffenbarung:
Suche des grossen Rätsels Lösung.

In the vast unmeasured world-wide spaces,
In the endless stream of time,
In the depths of human soul-life,
In the world's great revelations:
Seek the unfolding of life's great mystery.

The lines are related in such a way that the first four lines have an element of expectation which finds its fulfilment in the fifth line.

Let us now go back to another speech exercise:

Protzig preist	Proxy prized
Bäder brünstig	bather broomstick
Polternd putzig	polka pushing
Bieder bastelnd	beady basket
Puder patzend	prudent pertness
Bergig brüstend	bearskin bristled

You can learn a great deal from this.

Now we shall repeat the exercise:

Dass er dir log uns darf es nicht loben
Dart may these boats through darkening gloaming

Now something similar, but having a slight emotive element. There are four lines to which I would like to draw your attention. I shall dictate them to you afterwards. The emotive element should be brought to expression particularly in the first line:

Lalle Lieder lieblich	Lulling leader limply
Lipplicher Laffe	liplessly laughing
Lappiger lumpiger	loppety lumpety
Laichiger Lurch	lackety lout

Imagine that you have a green frog before you that stares at you with its mouth open and you speak to it in the last three lines. But in the first line you ask of it that it should 'sing sweet songs'. You must say this first line with humorous affection, as if you were making demands on it.

And now another piece of prose, a fable.

Die Eiche

Der rasende Nordwind hatte seine Stärke in einer stürmischen Nacht an einer erhabenen Eiche bewiesen. Nun lag sie gestreckt. Eine Menge niedriger Sträuche lagen unter ihr zerschmettert. Ein Fuchs, der seine Grube nicht weit davon hatte, sah sie des Morgens darauf. 'Was für ein Baum', rief er. 'Hatte ich doch nimmermehr gedacht, dass er so gross gewesen wäre.'

The Oak

One stormy night the raging north wind pitted its strength against a magnificent oak, which now lay on the ground. A number of low bushes lay shattered beneath it. A fox, whose lair was not far away, saw it next morning. 'What a tree!' he cried. 'I would never have thought it had been so big.'

In what does the moral of this fable lie?

A participant in the course: That one only notices at death how great a person was.

Another participant: That a smaller person only notices what a greater one was when he has fallen.

Rudolf Steiner: But why is the fox, who is cunning, brought in?

A participant: Because the fox's cunning does not come anywhere near the grandeur of the tree.

Rudolf Steiner: In which sentence would the moral of the fable lie in connection with the fox's cunning? 'I would never have thought it had been so big.'

He had simply never looked up, he had always only looked at it from below, had only gone round it below, and there the tree took up little space. Despite his cunning he had only seen what one sees of the circumference from below.

I would like to draw your attention to the fact that fables which take place in the world of fable may be read realistically, but poems never.

*

Speech Exercise:

Nimm mir nicht, was, wenn ich freiwillig dir es reiche, dich beglückt
Deprive me not of what, when I give it to you freely, pleases you.

Rudolf Steiner: The sentence is given for phrasing according to meaning. First you have the short clause: *Nimm mir nicht* and also the clause: *was dich beglückt*, which is, however, interrupted by the clause: *wenn ich freiwillig dir es reiche*. This has to be brought out in speaking. You must see that you take up the same intonation again for *dich beglückt* as that which you had when you left off at the word *was*.

Speech Exercises:

Redlich ratsam	Rateless ration
Rüstet rühmlich	roosted roomily
Riesig rächend	reason wretched
Ruhig rollend	ruined Roland
Reuige Rosse	royalty roster

Nimm nicht Nonnen in nimmermüde Mühlen
Name neat Norman on nimble moody mules

Pfiffig pfeifen	Piffling fifer
Pfäffische Pferde	prefacing feather
Pflegend Pflüge	phlegma fluting
Pferchend Pfirsiche	fairground piercing

Verse for the last week in August from the *Calendar of the Soul*:

Ich fühle fruchtend fremde Macht
Sich stärkend mir mich selbst verleihn,
Den Keim empfind ich reifend
Und Ahnung lichtvoll weben
Im Innern an der Selbstheit Macht.

I feel a power unwonted bearing fruit,
Gather its strength and lend myself to me.
I sense the germ maturing,
The while my boding weaves a web of light
Within me for my selfhood's power.*

---

* Translation by A. C. Harwood in *The Meditative Year* (Rudolf Steiner Press, London, 1972).

Speech Exercises:

Pfiffig pfeifen aus Näpfen
Pfäffische Pferde schlüpfend
Pflegend Pflüge hüpfend
Pferchend Pfirsiche knüpfend

Kopfpfiffig pfeifen aus Näpfen
Napfpfäffische Pferde schlüpfend
Wipfend pflegend Pflüge hüpfend
Tipfend pferchend Pfirsiche knüpfend

The pf must be made really gymnastically active.

The following is a piece in which attention must be paid partly to the form and partly to the content:

Das Gebet

Galgenlied von Christian Morgenstern

Die Rehlein beten zur Nacht,
Hab acht!
Halb neun!
Halb zehn!
Halb elf!
Halb zwölf!
Zwölf!
Die Rehlein beten zur Nacht,
Hab acht!
Sie falten die kleinen Zehlein,
Die Rehlein.

The Does' Prayer*

Gallows Song by Christian Morgenstern

The does, as the hour grows late,
Med-it-ate;
Med-it-nine;
Med-i-ten;
Med-eleven;

---

* Translation by Max Knight, University of California Press, Berkeley and Los Angeles 1964.

Med-twelve;
Mednight!
The does, as the hour grows late,
Meditate.
They fold their little toesies,
the doesies.

*

Rudolf Steiner: The following exercises are designed to make the speech organs flexible:

Ketzer petzten jetzt kläglich	Curtsey Betsy jets cleric
Letztlich leicht skeptisch	lastly light sceptic
Zuwider zwingen zwar	Tu-whit twinkle 'twas
Zweizweckige Zwacker zu wenig	twice twigged tweaker
Zwanzig Zwerge	to twenty twangy twirlings
Die sehnige Krebse	the zinnia crisper
Sicher suchend schmausen	zither zooming shambles
Dass schmatzende Schmachter	this smartened smacking
Schmiegsam schnellstens	smuggler sneezing
Schnurrig schnalzen	snoring snatching.

This kind of exercise only reaches perfection when it is learnt by heart.

From: *Wir fanden einen Pfad* by Christian Morgenstern (R. Piper Verlag, Munich, 1915).

Wer vom Ziel nicht weiss,
Kann den Weg nicht haben,
Wird im selben Kreis
All sein Leben traben;
Kommt am Ende hin,
Wo er hergerückt,
Hat der Menge Sinn
Nur noch mehr zerstückt.

*

Speech Exercises:

Ketzer krächzer petzten jetzt kläglich	Curtsey cressets Betsy jets cleric
Letztlich plötzlich leicht skeptisch	lastly plotless light sceptic

These exercises will only come right if you can reel them off by heart.

Nur renn nimmer reuig	Narrow wren mirror royal
Gierig grinsend	gearing grizzled
Knoten knipsend	noting nippers
Pfänder knüpfend	fender coughing

From: *Wir fanden einen Pfad* by Christian Morgenstern

Wer vom Ziel nicht weiss,
Kann den Weg nicht haben,
Wird im selben Kreis
All sein Leben traben;
Kommt am Ende hin,
Wo er hergerückt,
Hat der Menge Sinn
Nur noch mehr zerstückt.

Wer vom Ziel nichts kennt,
Kann's doch heut erfahren;
Wenn es ihn nur brennt
Nach dem Göttlich-Wahren:
Wenn in Eitelkeit
Er nicht ganz versunken
Und vom Wein der Zeit
Nicht bis oben trunken.

Rudolf Steiner: We shall only be able to observe the different nuances of these two verses after the third verse has been read tomorrow.

*

Speech Exercise:

Klipp plapp plick glick	clip plop pluck cluck
Klingt Klapperrichtig	clinked clapper richly
Knatternd trappend	knotted trappings
Rossegetrippel	rosily tripled

From: *Wir fanden einen Pfad* by Christian Morgenstern. Free prose rendering by Nancy Hummel.

Wer vom Ziel nicht weiss,	He who does not know of the goal
Kann den Weg nicht haben.	cannot be on the right path,
Wird im selben Kreis	He will tread round the same circle
All sein Leben traben;	his whole life through;
Kommt am Ende hin,	He will arrive in the end at the
Wo er hergerückt,	point from which he started,
Hat der Menge Sinn	But with his common sense even
Nur noch mehr zerstückt	more fragmented.
Wer vom Ziel nichts kennt,	He who knows nothing of the goal
Kann's doch heut erfahren;	can learn of it today,
Wenn es ihn nur brennt	If only he has a burning thirst
Nach dem Göttlich-Wahren;	for things divine and true;
Wenn in Eitelkeit	If he has not been claimed
Er nicht ganz versunken	completely by vanities,
Und vom Wein der Zeit	And has not drunk to the full
Nicht bis oben trunken.	the wine of the present age.
Denn zu fragen ist	For we needs must ask
Nach den stillen Dingen.	about all silent things,
Und zu wagen ist,	And venture if we want to win
Will man Licht erringen;	through to the light;
Wer nicht suchen kann,	He who cannot seek
Wie nur je ein Freier,	like an ardent suitor
Bleibt im Trugesbann	Will remain entangled in the
Siebenfacher Schleier. *	deception of seven-fold veils.

*

* Notes of indications announced the previous day are not available.

Speech Exercises:

Schlinge Schlange geschwinde	Slinging slanging a swindler
Gewundene Fundewecken weg	the wounding fooled a victor vexed
Gewundene Fundewecken	The wounding fooled a swindler
Geschwinde schlinge Schlange weg	slinging slanging vexed.
Marsch schmachtender	March smarten ten
Klappriger Racker	clap rigging rockets
Krackle plappernd linkisch	crackling plopping lynxes
Flink von vorne fort	fling from forward forth
Krackle plappernd linkisch	crackling plopping lynxes
Flink von vorne fort	fling from forward forth
Marsch schmachtender	march smarten ten
Klappriger Racker	clap rigging rockets

Rudolf Steiner on the last exercise: Good to start with. One person begin, then the next one continue.*

---

* In connection with these exercises we would refer to the fourteenth lecture in: *The Study of Man* (Rudolf Steiner Press, London, 1966).

RUDOLF STEINER

COURSE ON THE ART OF SPEECH FORMATION 1922

PART I

RECORDED BY MARIE STEINER

All teaching in declamation and recitation should be of a kind that allows the pupil to find his way into the very art of speech formation itself, into what reverberates in the soul from speech formation. It should bring the pupil to the point of being able to hear correctly. To a person who is capable of really hearing correctly what poetry has to reveal, correct breathing, correct bearing and the mechanics will come by themselves as a kind of resonance to the correct hearing. It is all-important to allow the pupil himself to live in the element of declamation and recitation and to leave everything else to him. He must surrender to what is objectively tonal, musical, pictorial, to what lives in a really poetic form. It is only by bringing the pupil to the point of developing – if I may express myself paradoxically – a correct aural feeling for what has been declaimed for him and, through this, a correct sensitivity for what moves spiritually on the waves of what his aural feeling conveys to him, that he will draw to himself what he has felt vibrating around him. He perceives this (it is an illusion but it must nevertheless be cultivated) so to speak in his surroundings. Only through certain verbal sequences that are formed artistically in such a way that they correspond with the human organism; only by reciting such verbal sequences should one learn to give shape and form to the breath and to everything else in the way of 'attitude'. Only then shall we be adequate for all that stems from our elevated Goethean view of art and our sensitivity for art.

RUDOLF STEINER

I would like to add, in connection with what has already been said,* that you must try to work back upon the cultivation of the voice through the sounds. You must learn to react inwardly to the light vowels, for instance E (eh) and I (ee), in a different way from the dark ones A (ah), O (oh), U (oo), AU (ow). The dark vowels A (ah), O (oh), U (oo), AU (ow) are of a kind that arise in placid people living predominantly in the blood, while E (eh) and I (ee) arise in those who are emotional and excitable.

It is particularly important that you allow the subtler differentiations of E (eh) and I (ee) to work upon the organism. You consolidate speech when you use the vowel E (eh) in training, especially in that restrained manner of speaking in which the main idea is to express oneself, reveal oneself, rather than to listen. It is then that the stream of speech is driven back into the nervous system.† This is the vowel which best expresses an established train of thought and works most directly, like a dictum. It is a favourite sound in monologues where you speak to yourself with no one listening. People who brood within themselves usually like E (eh) most of all. Hence E (eh) is of the greatest importance for the consolidation of the speech organs and it is good to use it in training.

For example:

> *Lebendige Wesen treten wesendes Leben*
> Lay bending various trays facing day's labour

One must calm oneself.
First rendering:

> *Lebende Wesen treten wesendes Leben*

---

* The exercises practised in the courses held in the summer and autumn of 1922 are now familiar to the reader and are therefore not printed here. In 1921 Rudolf Steiner gave them to some lecturers, and we have therefore printed them again in the context of the *Contributions to the Art of Lecturing* (p. 185).

† These last two sentences were inserted by Rudolf Steiner into Marie Steiner's manuscript.

If you say this a hundred times in a fortnight you will see that it will help you more than any mechanical placing of speech. If you allow your speech organs to run through these wave-like movements you drive nerve force into your speech organs.

Whilst recognizing that the sound E (eh) has the tendency to develop the nerve-life in contrast to the blood-life, the sound I (ee) on the other hand leads the nerve stream outwards again. Thus you will see that your nerve force works outwards when you say I (ee). When the speech organs work with I (ee) your speech takes on a quality of conviction rather than of inwardness.

You will really achieve something if you say the E (eh) after the I (ee):

Wirklich findig wird Ich im irdischen Lebenswesen
Quickly finished veered each it irritates labour's phases.

A state of excitement goes over into a state of calm. You can feel exactly how a mounting nerve stream runs into the organs of speech.

You must reverse this:

Im irdischen Lebenswesen wird Ich wirklich findig
It irritates labour's phases veered each quickly finished

At first the flow of speech is driven inwards and then it turns outwards again.

If you add the E (eh) to the I (ee) and notice how the I (ee) is affected, you will see that through the addition of the E (eh) the nerve stream is held back and consolidated.

Die Liebestriebe werte nicht gering
These leafless trees awaken in the spring

The E (eh) approaches the I (ee). When the E (eh) is mingled with the I (ee) the stream is stemmed and results in the consolidation of the speech organs.

This replaces a mechanical means of placing speech.

If you let this go through you a hundred times in a fortnight you will stimulate aright the stream which should flow through you.

The nerves should now find the right support in the neighbouring organs, for instance in fat. The vowel EI (i as in high) tends to make one fat. If the training is to be balanced it is necessary to work towards a consolidation and an expansion of the nerve stream.

This will be achieved through the following exercise:

Breite weise Wiesen über das Land
Brighter wider wielding over this land

It is an expanding of oneself. Thus the possibility arises, through the forming of the sounds themselves, of achieving the necessary adjustment of the speech organs.

We learn to breath correctly by letting a number of well-placed sounds run through the speech organs, training them in this way. In doing this by means of sounds everyone acquires his own individual character and develops his own inherent nature.

*

In declaiming and reciting it can be of assistance to bear in mind the '*valeurs*', the true worth of the vowels. It is altogether necessary that you learn to become aware of this way of forming speech in declaiming, and in speaking in general. If, for example, you wish to study a dialogue, you must know how it has been built up according to the formative forces of speech. Let us assume that we have a placid person and an excitable one. Good poets often make this contrast. But you will notice that really good poets characterize the calm person and the excitable one through the very sounds themselves. The reciter must have a feeling for this and must consider especially those vowels that correspond more to the calm character or to the excitable one. Exercises such as those given below are necessary in order to develop this feeling.

Let us suppose the one person, who lives predominantly in the blood-organization, and who does not easily fly off the handle, is inwardly firm and calm. The other is a person who lives on his nerves, flies off the handle at the slightest provocation, and is excitable and fidgety.

The vowels which bring to expression what lives within the placid person are A (ah), U (oo), O (oh), AU (ow). In a text where other vowels are present these in particular must be remembered and allowed to sound more fully.

The vowels of the nerve-person are I (ee) and E (eh) and these come of themselves to his tongue. Conclusions can be drawn in the languages of different peoples as to racial characteristics from the preponderance of the one or the other vowel. It is possible to study how A (ah) and O (oh) predominate in nations of a quiet and stable disposition, and E (eh) and I (ee) in excitable ones.

One must of course bear in mind that even Lichtenberg,* who lived many decades ago, declared with a certain justification that there were ninety-nine percent more poets and writers than were necessary for the good of mankind.

But a reciter can do much if he emphasizes the one thing and not the other, giving resonance to the words of the placid person and sharply accentuating those of the fidgety one.

1. The placid person:

   Sahst du das Blass an Wang und Mund?
   Marked you the pallor of that countenance?

2. The nervous one:

   Nichts im Gesicht bemerkte ich.
   I didn't see anything strange in his face.

The nerves vibrate involuntarily with these sounds.

1. *Du kannst nur schauen, was krass.*
   You must look rather at what is crass.

Here the blood must be kept calm.

* Georg Christoph Lichtenberg (1742–1799).

2. *Nimm mir nicht mich selbst.*
   Take not my feelings of self from me.
The nervous one.

1. *Allzustark wachst du kaum.*
   Hardly enough on guard are you.

2. *Eben deswegen will ich dies nicht.*
   I will not take it that you say this!

If you want to speak out of your whole feeling you must pay attention to your speech with your whole feeling.

Take for example the word *Wagen* (cart). One *Wagen* is something solid, contained within itself. In the word *Wägen* (carts) the contours are less defined, they become diffuse. In dialect we find a different phenomenon – the A (ah) goes over into the O (oh) – the peasant says in the singular *Wog'n*; it becomes even more solid. For the peasant *die Wagen* signifies several; the O (oh) lightens up in A (ah). You must therefore feel whether it grows dimmed or lighter. The sound becomes lighter because the object is dispersed, for example: *Baum* (tree), *Bäume* (trees). You must learn to feel your way into the sound.*

Take the word *mächtig* (powerful). There you have a definite feeling. But modern man no longer feels *Macht* (might). *Macht* is lost to him. On the other hand he often feels it unpleasant when a child, for example, is noisy. He wishes to quieten the child: *s(c)h . . . s(c)h. . . .* If you dim the word *mächtig* with this sound you get *Schmächtig* (slender). In this way you can develop an understanding for sounds, in contrast to an understanding of meaning.

There is something lying in most words which one can rightly bring out when declaiming if one knows, for example, that with

---

* At this point Dr. Steiner referred to his essay *Speech and the Genius of Language*, which is included in the second part of this book.

some one might blush, with others grow pale. In *Weinen* (to weep) lies an inner warding off of grief.

Wein: The word has something which, in a social sense, reminds one of *Betrübtsein* (grieved). Here you see the creative activity of the inner genius of language.

Let us go on. We have *Wein . . . s(c)h . . . Schwein* (pig). In grasping this one has the right undertone in speech. It is important to have felt what a sound does when it combines with others.

Let us take the word *Mar* (tale). We know it in connection with the word *Nachtmar* (nightmare). We find it again in *Mären* (tales): '*Uns ist in alten maeren wunders vil geseit – von heleden lobebaeren, von grôzer arebeit. . . .*'

In olden times these songs were spoken while striding up and down. Within this sound lies something of the feeling: I will present something which is in movement and which I can follow. – You find this again in the word *Marsch* (march off).

*

Imagine yourself to be an inherently proud person, not blessed with this world's goods. You come to someone who is, and who lets you feel his superiority, which perhaps stems only from his social standing. You lose your temper and insult him. You complain of this to a friend, who disapproves and calls upon you to make amends.

> *Wahr ist't – ich habe ihn beleidigt*
> *Kann man mir's verübeln?*
> *Kaum trat ich in sein Haus*
> *– Noch war die Türe nicht zu –*
> *Traf mich schon sein verachtender Blick.*

> True it is, I have offended him.
> Can you blame me for it?
> Hardly was I in the house
> – The door was not yet to –
> Stung me then his most scornful look.

In this exercise you have the opportunity of forming speech, out of the actual situation. It is necessary that you learn to form speech comprehensively.

You have five lines here. The first presents an actual fact, the second a situation in which you seek to justify yourself, the third a plea, the fourth a general explanation, and the fifth a continuation of the plea.

The next five lines are constructed in a similar way in order to bring the situation home.

> *Nun ja – ich will's wieder gutmachen*
> *Doch darf ich dann auch glauben,*
> *Dass er den Stachel mir nimmt*
> *– Wie können Blicke doch stechen –*
> *Der sich mir tief in die Seele bohrte?*

> Ah, well, I'll make it good again!
> But can I also hope
> that he'll retract his sharpness.
> – how far harsh looks can stab one –
> It bored deep down into my soul.

In the first line you make a slight admission and then you direct attention back to yourself. Reflection. In the second and third lines, you have a questioning sentence and a situation in which you try to carry on the plea; in the fourth, a musing on a general rule, a general explanation, and in the fifth, a return to the previous questioning sentence.

In this way a great deal will form itself.

Between these two parts lies the friend's answer:

> *Lerne doch das Leben nehmen, wie es ist.*
> *Siehst du das Elend jener Menschen nicht,*
> *Die weltfremd Entschlüsse fassen*
> *– Das Herz gar manches verführt den Kopf –*
> *Und die statt zu gehen stets stolpern?*

> Learn to take this life a bit more as it is!
> Don't you see the misery of people everywhere
> Who in their ignorance make mistaken decisions?
> – Many a heart misleads the head –
> And they, instead of progressing, forever stumble.

Learn to form the words sculpturally. Mere musical speaking does not of itself suffice. A beautiful voice alone still has something of an animalistic nature. It is necessary to shape speech.

The dramatic element must indeed lie in the actual formation of the sentence, not in the drama:

> *Hast du* doch *dies Buch gelesen?* ,
> Hast *du doch dies Buch* gelesen!

The other wanted to prevent him from doing so:

> *Hast du meinen Rat in den Wind geschlagen?*
> *Hast du* doch *dies Buch gelesen?*

With a certain irony:

> *Du solltest darüber etwas wissen!*
> Hast *du doch dies Buch* gelesen!

If we try to transfer the conscious handling of the instruments of speech to the management of sound formation, then we shall realize how mistaken it is to set out from a purely physiological standpoint. Nowadays people try to train the voice through the manipulation of muscles and so forth. It is not right to set out from a physiological adjustment of the organs in the search for the sound. This never leads to a natural functioning of the speech organs. Speaking must proceed from hearing and, indeed, from hearing oneself. You must learn to hear yourself when you say an mm or an nn or an ll. In this case hearing is not quite the same as in ordinary life. It is rather like feeling the sound, as if you took hold of something in chest and head which pours through the ears. If you remain sensitive you can feel the movements of the ear-drum. Thus speaking depends on hearing, and hearing is actually a feeling. Imagine also how the sound strikes against your ear: the ear-drum begins to vibrate. The oscillations starting from the mouth and sounding through the Eustachian tubes are equally important. They are grasped at first inwardly, but the ear resounds in sympathy. When someone else speaks the ear resounds more strongly. Hearing is always connected with the whole human being. It is as if you were in a globe of air and were watching what the air does when you are speaking. What takes place in the diaphragm, chest and head should take place unconsciously. You must learn everything that has to be learnt through the sound. The breath itself must be regulated unconsciously when one senses the sound and, in sensing, hears. What has to be done in order to speak the sound must be learnt from the sound itself. There should in no way be a feeling of using the larynx and other organs. One uses the air instead. It should grow into a habit to feel what the air does. The special quality of wave sounds, vibratory, impact and breath sounds should be felt. Listening must become a habit, above all listening to oneself, which in a certain respect is a feeling.

The rolling of the r must be felt in a different way from the undulating of the l. Learning to speak is something that is always based on the whole being of man. Finding a controlled relationship between the breath and the blood circulation – that is being able to recite.

The ratio between breath and blood circulation, four to one, is at the foundation of all prosody, poetry and everything else. The hexameter, first cultivated by the Greeks, was founded on the relationship between the breath and the pulse-beat. It is the archetypal verse measure based on the ratio of one to four. This is individual to each person. Four to one is only approximately correct and everyone must find the measure through his own feeling. (It is similar to the laws according to which the flower grows, laws which, however, are also taken up into the feeling through spiritual cognition. Spiritual cognition is just as living as nature itself.) Each breath we draw has four pulse-beats. Through spiritual awareness the Greeks were able to perceive this. They created in the hexameter a copy of this primal rhythm: three dactyls, caesura, three dactyls, pause, corresponding to four pulse-beats and again four pulse-beats, or the drawing of two breaths.

$$- \cup \cup \ - \cup \cup \ - \cup \cup \ | \ - \cup \cup \ - \cup \cup \ - \cup \cup \ |$$

Thus the hexameter is based on the rhythm of the human breath. For this reason all manipulation of the diaphragm and so forth is useless. Human nature does this of its own accord and learns from speech.

*

Try to feel the differentiations when you practise the following exercise:

> *Sturm-Wort rumort um Tor und Turm*
> *Molch-Wurm bohrt durch Tor und Turm*
> *Dumm tobt Wurm-Molch durch Tor und Turm*
>
> Storm wolf roars forth though door and tomb
> Bold wolves bored through door and tomb
> Doom taught wolves bold through door and tomb

In the first sentence you can swim in the stream of the speech. The second is different, and the third quite different again. Try to make this difference in the flow of the speech, in swimming with it.

*

You almost learn to do vocal contortions when you practise the following exercise:

Abracadabra
Rabadacabra
Bradacaraba
Cadarabraba

You learn everything through A (ah). Just transpose the syllables. You can experience whole worlds within these variations. The voice slips snugly into them.

*

Speaking vowels means pouring forth one's inner world into the stream of speech.

Speaking consonants means moulding fluidity, casting it into form. Speaking consonants means living together with the world.

Speaking vowels means expressing one's inner world.

Speaking consonants: the reciprocal relationship of man to the world.

*

In order to learn to feel what lies within the sounds I can recommend a simple meditation on cube and globe. Imagine that someone wanted to make you spit out a ball. Then you would utter the sound d. Speaking the sound d means protecting yourself against something; then you spit out this round thing, this ball. D is round. – You must spit out the cube with k. You must acquire a feeling for rounding-off a sound or making it angular.

What lies in A (ah)? A marvelling. In E (eh)? A pushing away of something.

The vowels express our impulses of will and feeling, the consonants more our concepts. Speaking in consonants means living in the outer world and taking part in it. Speaking in vowels means expressing one's inner life. In a play, if I wish to form what belongs to the outer world I shall heap up the consonants. If I wish to form what is inward I shall heap up the vowels. Great poets pay attention to this.

*

Let us consider awhile the cultivation of speech by means of the sounds themselves.

To be learnt by actual practice are:

1. Distinctness of speech,
2. Fluidity of speech,

70

3. Enclosure of speech,
4. Membering of speech.

All these things must be learnt by the actual practice of the sounds themselves. Under *distinctness* we mean that the sound is to be formed in its entirety. In accustoming oneself during practice to speaking the s and the m properly we learn to form all other sounds. Through practising these sounds we learn to speak distinctly.

Do these simple exercises a hundred times in a fortnight and learn to find your way into clear speech:

Mäuse messen mein Essen   Moisten mason mine essence

Simply do this a hundred times in a fortnight and your voice will become distinct, so that the listener can distinguish one sound from another.

Then the voice must flow, and not be chopped up. The voice must be treated in such a way as to allow the breath-stream to flow. The *fluidity* of the voice can be brought about through finding one's way into l:

Lämmer leisten leises Läuten   Lamer lightness Liza loiters

Enclosure. By the enclosure of the voice I mean that the single sounds are not to be released into the world bare and unclothed. Everything that lives forms a skin around itself, even the smallest animal. The sound must do so too, so that it does not splutter out, nor goes out naked, but is clothed.

In b one acquires a feeling for the enclosing, the covering of the sound:

Bei biedern Bauern bleib brav   By beaten bowers bide brave

These feelings are achieved by entering into the sounds:

with m the feeling for distinctness,
with l the feeling for fluidity,
with b the feeling for enclosure.

Now we still have to consider *membering*. We must be in a position to divide up a sentence in such a way that the listener is spared the great effort of dividing it up for himself. The reciter must take care to see that the sentence goes into the ear. This is achieved by practising the k-exercises. Through such k-exercises one acquires a certain capacity to divide up the sentence. Failure to practise k-exercises leads to a lack of courage in inserting punctuation marks in the right way.

Komm kurzer kräftiger Kerl   Come crooked craftiest cur

Now I will go back to the exercise *Abracadabra* and give you its mantric meaning.

A long time ago, when people learnt to speak, they learnt mantric sacrificial verses. In the word *Abracadabra* there is a self-contained sound-structure. A (ah) is the primal sound which even the child learns to speak. A (ah) is the whole man. There is nothing in the human organism which does not vibrate with the A (ah). You can feel it in the tip of your little toe. It is the first total feeling that the child has. Therefore A (ah) was the sound spoken by those who had some understanding for the whole being of man.

B expresses the protective covering of man, the house in which he dwells. A snail is still able to move with his house, but a man cannot. So there is no movement yet as such in the A (ah).

A: is the whole man.
Ab: is man with his house.
Abr: Man walks with his house.
Abra: man walks with his house and creeps out of it.
Abrac: Man walks with his house, creeps out of it and places himself squarely there as man. The A (ah) comes again and again so that he may always remain man.
Abraca: he places himself squarely there and feels himself as man.
Abracad: he catches sight of another man.
Abracada: he points to him.
Abracadab: the other man also has a house.
Abracadabr: the other man also walks and has his house.
Abracadabra: that is a man like me.

In the sense of primeval speech you have therefore said: 'I as man feel myself in my house, walking, feel another man with his house, also walking. He is a man as I am.'

This was felt in the variations I have already cited.

Thus speech is learnt through forming the sounds and not through any adjustment of the organs.

✻

We will now see how the voice may be placed by means of the sounds, and how it becomes clear what we should learn through them.

In speaking the sounds t and d you will have a feeling which is localized in the front part of the mouth, on the tongue. You will notice, while speaking, something akin to a probing of what is being expressed. You will feel tentatively with these consonants what you speak. In doing this you grow intimately into a formation of speech, you have something which does not express thought intellectually. You must feel, as it were, sympathy and antipathy within the formation of the sound itself. I will give you an exercise for this. It is necessary to choose drastic examples because the feeling for sound is so blunted nowadays. Let us suppose you want to break through a door. . . . Nowadays one no longer feels what lies in the sounds, but one should train oneself to do so. T – a vigorous thrust with the tongue, a feeling of forceful contact. D – a gentler feeling.

Tritt dort die Türe durch   Trip dauntless the door of doom

Feel in each d-sound this touching, this contact, and in t a stronger contact.

You have a poem, and you want to present it in such a way that people can experience it to the fullest possible extent. This you can do in two ways. Think of someone who, for instance, wears a silk dress. You can look at it and delight in it or you can have a different impression. You can handle it and experience pleasure in this way. So you have had two experiences.

73

In a poem you can experience the prosaic words and work out the content or else you can experience its form through sound.

*

With the majority of people the voice lies too near the lips. Because of this the word can lie too far forward; then one has to send it further back.

> *Halt! Hebe hurtig hohe Humpen!*
> Halt, habit hoarding hollow hamper

You will give the words greater weight through using this region at the back. Then your words will gain a power which is more convincing. Through using this region at the back your words will acquire full force.

> *Hole Heinrich hierher hohe Halme*
> Wholly hindmost hear her hollow hammer

You cannot speak this if you trip along in front on the lips. You must therefore accustom yourself to studying words with regard to their formation. What I say applies to the German language. Each language has its own organic laws. In German there are words from which one can study what it means to live in the words. For instance: *Horch* (listen or hear). A whole world lies therein. The h in *horch* has the deepest possible foundation. In addition the word closes with ch, and the ch is laid into the whole breath. H moulds plastically, while ch (as in loch) goes right into things with the breath. H says: Listen . . . and go into what you hear. Absorb it.

Now experience how the human being flows over into something other than himself in the little word *Ich* (I) through which a grasping of that other comes to expression. *Happig – hab' ich* (have I) . . . Now compare this with such formations as *launig* (humorous), *sträflich* (punishable), *länglich* (longish). *Launig* means *der Laune gleich*; *ig* – like. One grows like unto all things in saying *ich* (I), which is the same as *ig*. My breath streams out and merges with all things; I become like unto all things.

What I say is not taken from etymology, philology or linguistics, but from speech formation.

It is essential to feel the sound-pictures in learning to recite.

Now imagine you want to bring someone from a state of rest into activity. Take the following sound-picture:

Pfeife pfiffige Pfeifer Pfiffe   Fie! fifer fifing piffling piffle

There is something in this which gives the other person a push. Feel the whole force of this pushing as it comes to expression in the little word: *Pfui*.

Then try to practise this in a gentler form:

Empfange empfindend Pfunde Pfeffer
Emphatic enfeebled folding feather

The sense is of no importance in these exercises. In disregarding the meaning the spirit of the sounds is discovered all the sooner. Those who learn to live in the sound receive cosmic revelations.

If you want to learn to speak to a person confidentially you can learn this from the s(c)h:

Schwinge schwere Schwalbe   Swinging swirling swallow
Schnell im Schwunge schmerzlos   shell in swooning, smirchless

(first version: *schnurrig* instead of *schmerzlos*)

The poet has a natural feeling for this, if he is one who places the sounds together in such a way; the reciter must cultivate his own feeling for sound from it.

Everything depends on the reciter finding the right attitude to speech, experiencing the poem. He must remember that the main experience must be one of forming the sounds. He must learn to experience the poetic element. If a Greek had been offered such recitation as is nowadays considered good, it would simply have made him nervous, strong as he was. He would not

75

have known whether one was being foolish or clever. The Greeks could experience language and had the fine feeling for sound-formation which we must regain on a conscious level.

Think of the scene in the Iliad where Achilles has murdered Hector, and Priam comes to lament:

Denn ich dulde, was nie ein Mensch auf Erden geduldet,
Mir an den Mund die Hand zu ziehen, die den Sohn mir gemordet.

Because I endure what no man on earth has endured,
To kiss the hand of him who murdered my son.

Can it not truly be said that Priam lives completely in this experience? The possibility of feeling one's way into the experience is there. – In m you move with the stream of speech.

✻

Today I will describe from a different aspect exercises for giving shape to the very being of speech. We must be quite clear that the speech organism is in a certain sense the whole man. In the first instance speech takes place as my own activity in the larynx and neighbouring organs, but the whole human being is involved. This becomes particularly clear if one takes speech as the basis for the artistic and poetic shaping of what lives in the human soul. In that he speaks, man makes use above all of the dim stirrings of life, which otherwise do not come to consciousness. These can be drawn up out of consciousness, in like manner as the fact that one grows. Within the child an activity takes place, as a result of which he grows. When the child learns to speak it is only a transference to the speech organs of what has been going on in the other organs hitherto. When the poetry of primeval times is understood, what lives within it as poetic formative force is little other than an activity of the forces of growth freed from the body. The presentation of epic poetry must be felt in this way. In this, man sets free the forces that are the least conscious. In the same way as that in which he grows, the human being is artistic in the realm of epic. Within the epic

76

stream we are especially active in the sounds formed chiefly through the palate, so we can acquire the epic style when we practise palatal sounds. And without becoming mystically ecstatic we can discern that when we practise the epic style with the palatal sounds we are working with our ether body. Practising palatal sounds means exerting the ether body.

I say this so that you may have the feeling that you must not theorize, but must train the body.

On the other hand when you consider the dramatic style you will no longer have the feeling that the dramatic element springs from the forces of growth. We encounter something else. The forces of sympathy and antipathy become active. This means that our astral body, the bearer of feelings and emotions, becomes active. And what emerges as the dramatic element is what is produced by the tongue. Later on we will recite passages in which there are many lingual sounds. In these there lives the vibration of the astral element. And in the works of sensitive poets you will notice how you feel the words like a taste on the tongue. You must learn to taste the dramatic.

Where our ego is engaged, where we go most of all to the surface of our organism, we have to do with the lyric style. There we must practise labial sounds. There our ego vibrates, our ego which gives itself up to the outer world. Try to feel how in p, b, v, the whole human being presses to the surface. Take v, that v that goes so much to the surface that the lips do not quite close, as with other labial sounds, but stay open. In speaking the v you will feel a vibrating and will sense the v on the whole surface. If a poet wishes to give you shivers down your spine he will do well to use a great many v sounds. With p, b, m, the lips touch each other, but with v there is a space in between.

One may observe that it is just in the German laguage that so much may be said about the inner value of sounds. In words such as *warm* (warm) you can really feel the way in which the soul lives within the word. In contrast, compare the word in the neo-Latin languages. In the neo-Latin languages the effect of the outer world on the human being is expressed when he is warm. In German it is the inner experience. Thus you have v which streams out, A (ah), then r which moves onward and last of all m, that labial sound which says one is aware of what lives within the word.

The German language is a language of the soul and therefore it is a pity that one only experiences it in the same way as the languages of the west. These are garments of man, whereas the German language, especially when grasped at the level where it still remains dialect, is through and through a language that is inwardly experienced. It is good, for this reason, to listen attentively to what lies within dialect in order to make progress in recitation. In southern Germany there is a word for lightning flashing in the distance (not summer lightning). In the word *Himmlitzer* the threefold zigzagging of the lightning is experienced and not only the swiftness of its flash.

So you must study:

The lyric style through the labial sounds,
the dramatic style through the lingual sounds,
the epic style through the palatal sounds.

When you feel that a certain passage is dramatic then you should stress the lingual sounds in your reciting.

Here I would recommend another exercise. Let us imagine you are dealing with a very boring person. If, remembering what he has said, you repeat it out loud stressing the lingual sounds (when he is not present, of course), you will find that what he has said is quite interesting and dramatic. It is just the same if you look at a deadly boring philosophical sentence. If you emphasize the labial sounds it will assume a lyric character.

It is altogether good to pay heed to such things, and to train through the organism of speech, independently of all meaning. For example:

Bei meiner Waffe	By miner wafer
Sie Vieh schieden	see fee shielding
Nur erlag Inger ich	noon air lark anger ink

You go backwards from the lips: f s v s(c)h d. Then right back: *nur erlag Inger ich*. In such exercises you will notice how r has three different placings, which must be practised in this way.

*

When through practising in the right way you allow the consonantal element to work in you, you will ultimately bring the whole human speech organism into a right configuration. Naturally you cannot bring out the meaning of language immediately, because in speech the sense is only of secondary importance. In order to understand better what is meant here, let us take an example from primitive laguages which appear to have merely an undertone of sense. Here the endeavour is to let the stream of speech flow just as it wills. The poet also tries to do this, for fundamentally he strives to emancipate the speech stream from abstraction.

Bei meiner Waffe	By miner wafer
Sie Vieh schieden	see fee shielding
Nur erlag Inger ich	noon air lark anger ink

In speaking this, you will notice that you begin to speak in front, in the region of the lips. The vowels here play no role, they are only there as padding.

Externally the resonance rises to the crest of a wave and then recedes again.

So you go from the formation of the labials to the control of the dentals, and from there to the formation of the lingual and palatal sounds. In doing this you move from the front to the back.

When you do the following:

Ich ringe Groll	Ink ringer growl
Rind war beim Baum	reeled far by boom

it is so that you have: *ich ringe Gro* . . . in the region of the palate, *oll Rind* on the tongue and *war beim Baum* on the lips.

You go from the back toward the front.

First I go back towards myself, then forward out of myself.

The consonants are arranged in such a way that you can follow their path in the formation of speech from the front to the back and again from the back to the front.

In my example you will find that your attention is drawn immediately to the passage from the front to the back.

With the exception of the dental zone you find the r everywhere and finally in the palatal region again. This is because there are three r's; a labial r, a lingual r and a palatal r.

When you do exercises such as these you will be stimulated as a matter of course to give the r the right colouring. From this you will see that the r has a different character from the other consonants.

The human being becomes quite wild in the r, he is beside himself. R can roll everywhere. Man is always beyond himself in

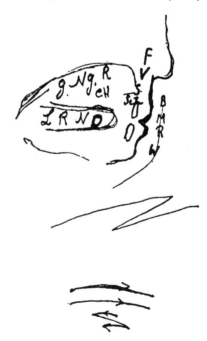

From one of Rudolf Steiner's notebooks

the r, while in the h and ch he remains in himself, even in the surrender of ch. With h as with the vowels, we draw the astral body entirely back into the organism of speech.

When one holds to these things one finds how meaning enters into speech as by a kind of leap.

When we do not check this process, which is determined by our organism, meaning comes into speech.

Ich ringe gross Schaf	Ink ringer grows shaft
Voll Rind nieder beim Weih	full reeled needy by vie

Ich ringe	from the palate
gross Schaf	to the teeth omitting the tongue
voll Rind nieder	back to the tongue
beim Weih	then the lips

Note the curve in the diagram opposite.

This is what gradually brings meaning into speech. You train yourself through such exercises.

The poet goes back to what the speech organs demand. For example:

Und es wallet and siedet und brauset und zischt

It progresses from tongue to teeth to lips, back to the tongue, to teeth, tongue, lips again, back to the teeth, back to the tongue, a small step forwards and then start again.

The poet tries in a certain sense to make use of the course that lies in the speech organs themselves. First fuller movements are made and then shorter ones. The meaning, which moves further and further away from the musical element, arises through the curves becoming ever more intricate. Hard by these curves lies the musical and sculptural element of language.

Let us go through the scene in the spirit realm,* not

---

* Scene 7 from *The Portal of Initiation*, Mystery Play by Rudolf Steiner (Steiner Book Centre, Toronto, 1973). See also the exercise on pages 118/119.

mystically, but in the light of speech formation. I have tried the following in it: *erglitzernd – klingen, erklingend – glitzern*, palatal sounds g and k, labial sound l; moving continually from the palate to the tongue and back again from the tongue to the palate. Therefore this peculiar ball-like movement works in speech because it always closes on itself again. Then the meaning is warranted through this formation.

We must ask the world's pardon because poetry has meaning, and through speech formation the reciter must beg forgiveness. These are the rules of human decency towards the cosmos.

*

The following can serve as transition to dramatic speaking. In our last lessons we considered how the consonants work into the organism of speech, training it. The reciter must consciously take note of what is happening in him through labial, lingual, dental and palatal sounds, and then he should transform this into a kind of mood. One also prepares the mood for recitation and declamation through speech itself, in a similar way.

If you look out a poem that makes you use your lips, especially one that has many labial sounds, you gain the possibility of calling forth a lyrical mood. By the use of labial sounds you will also acquire the right shade of speaking for the so-called objective lyric which appears often in Goethe's works, and in the use of which Martin Greif was especially a master.

What is objective lyric? Almost description, and yet lyric. An objective lyric is one that strongly approaches description in which the poet does not squeeze out his own emotions, but where something akin to Goethe's *Wanderers Nachtlied* (Wanderer's Night Song) rings out: *Über allen Gipfeln ist Ruh.*

The whole feeling this time is magically woven into a description and it can best be recited if it is spoken in such a way that the mood of the language of labial sounds predominates. It is not for nothing that *Liebe* (love) has a lingual and a labial sound. And even if you take the rather more rugged form of love which lies in the Latin *amor* you still have a labial sound in m, and the r must remain as a labial sound if it is to be inwardly justified.

You will be able to practise still another mood if you observe the interplay that takes place between the tongue and the other speech organs. This brings you into the dramatic mood, but if you try to prepare the mood through the palatal sounds you get the epic style, in which everything that a person utters must have already been inwardly assimilated.

In this way you must look for a passage rich in labials as preparation for the lyric style, a passage rich in linguals as preparation for the dramatic style, and a passage rich in palatal sounds as preparation for the epic style.

It is really true that the lips drive the innermost being of man quite consciously outwards. The astral body hovers on the lips and this alone makes it tolerable if the innermost being is to be given utterance at all.

On the other hand the tongue is the soul's organ of touch, and even physiologically the following is correct: If we are talking with two or three people our tongue feels whether the person concerned scolds, praises or blames us, and we want immediately to make a reply. This belongs to the dramatic mood.

It is especially interesting to notice how in epic the content has to be previously digested, and how even what one speaks from the tongue must turn towards the palate in order to bring out the epic shading.

In the same way the sounds that stream out from the lips in the lyric mood must be spoken further back physically in the epic, as if you think of the inner man as being external and then you speak into yourself. For example:

Es stand in alten Zeiten ein Schloss, so hoch und hehr . . .
There stood in olden times a castle, so great and noble . . .

You should always have the feeling here that the lips withdraw.

And from this standpoint if you declaim *Das Lied vom braven Mann* (The song of the good man) you will notice how you feel tempted to point the lips:

Hoch klingt das Lied vom braven Mann,
Wie Orgelton und Glockenklang.
Wer hohen Muts sich rühmen kann,
Den lohnt nicht Gold, den lohnt Gesang.
Gottlob! dass ich singen und preisen kann,
Zu singen und preisen den braven Mann.

High resounds the song of the good man,
As organ-tone, or the sound of bells.
He who is famed for high courage
Is rewarded not with gold, but with song,
God be praised that I can sing and praise,
To sing the praises of the good man.

On the other hand where the poem turns to epic you will be tempted to 'withdraw' the lips:

Der Tauwind kam vom Mittagsmeer
Und schnob durch Welschland trüb und feucht;
Die Wolken flogen vor ihm her,
Wie wenn der Wolf die Herde scheucht.
Er fegte die Felder, zerbrach den Forst;
Auf Seen und Strömen das Grundeis borst.

The wind came off the southern sea
And blew through Italy, turbid and damp,
The clouds flew before it,
As when the wolf frightens the flock.
It swept the fields, broke the forest,
On the lakes and streams the ground-ice cracked.

For the rest I would advise you to avoid the 'cheap-Jack' passages in Bürger's ballad. Leave out bad lyric and keep to good epic.*

*

---

* In a book used by Rudolf Steiner, *Deklamatorium, eine Mustersammlung ernster und heiterer Vortragsdichtungen aus der Weltliteratur,* published by Maximilian Bern in the Reclam edition, the first, ninth, eleventh, seventeenth and the last verse have for that reason been crossed out by him.

Before one can retrain the voice for the fully dramatic sphere, one must learn to use it much more consciously. Now that we have cultivated the stream of speech through the sounds themselves I would like to bring you into the situation of being able to feel the sounds still more consciously. You must remember that the sounds move between A (ah) and U (oo). Why? If you are to say A (ah) correctly you must open the glottis at the back as wide as possible. It is in a sense the primal sound. The A (ah) movement is that to which the light colours in the outer world most closely correspond. And besides, looking at the light colours tempts man most of all to open his mouth. You will often see Greek statues with a slightly opened mouth. The Greeks found this beautiful, because the Greeks in ancient times could not yet see dark colours such as blue in the same way as we do. The Greeks saw the sky as greenish in colour, lighter – hence the slight opening of the mouth.

And the sound in which the mouth and the space between the upper and lower teeth are most closed, so that the lips are pointed and the sound is prevented from coming out, is the U (oo). Between these two extremes lie all the other sounds.

The Greeks spoke A (ah) best of all, and worst of all U (oo). Humanity learnt to speak U (oo) in the course of its development. If the teeth are less open and the oral cavity somewhat smaller than with A (ah) you say E (eh). If you then make the oral cavity still smaller than with E (eh), and bring the lips still closer together, you get I (ee). If you go on to the O (oh) you must go closer to the lips, which are pointed. You form a circle with the lips, which are pointed. The lips are drawn together most of all with U (oo).

For example, if you say:

Lalle im Oststurm   Laughter in toadstool

you pass from the widest opening of the mouth to the most pronounced forward-pointing of the lips. It is strange that if you regard the vowels in this way you will find that I (ee) is the one which is most labile. The vowels A (ah) and U (oo) are more

85

defined and the easiest to form. For this reason the child learns to say A (ah) first of all, then U (oo), and then I (ee) – I (ee) last of all because it is the vowel requiring the most inner effort. It is in the middle, between wide-opened mouth and pointed lips. The sound I (ee) is plastic and configurated. The speaker should take these things seriously and become conscious of the different positions.

I have noticed that some people find it difficult to give the right nuance to the modified vowels. As an exercise the following combination of sounds will be helpful:

> *Lalle im Ost* (leave out *Sturm*)
> *Gänöbü*
> *Uf*

*

I have spoken of the way in which sound formation plays even into the moods of epic, dramatic and lyric poetry. The connection between what one speaks and what works in man as the mechanical and dynamic element may be learned from speech itself. One should never start off with the mechanical.

It is essential to have faith in one's own organism and to allow it to adjust itself properly through correct speaking, so that it finds its bearings in a manner that leads to this correct speaking, just as in the unfolding of the forces of growth there is as yet no disturbing interference from outside. During the time when man is not yet able to think he prepares his physical body in a wonderful way. It would disturb him very much if he were to be lectured on how he should adjust the lobe of his ear etc. so as to hear correctly. He has to follow a path already laid down by human nature. Speech has its own genius but these things must be brought to consciousness according to the stage of development of humanity.

It is good to discover how to treat the differences between

labial ⎫
lingual ⎬ sounds
palatal ⎭

so as to follow up the path taken within the organism. At first it is essential to practise everything in the most regular way possible. I shall give you exercises here whose meaning I shall explain later. Practising must become similar to speaking at lower levels, as in country dialects.

Bei seiner Gartentüre sass er	There by my new garden door he sat
Er hat dir geraten	He had advised you
Befolge nur aufs beste	'Carry out undaunted,
Recht vom Herzen gut	with an eager heart –
Sowie du nur gerade vermagst	as well indeed as you are able,
Rechten Rat	right resolves'!

You will find how easy it is to speak this exercise with fullness and distinctness if you try to speak, feeling and probing your way, with sculpturally rounded and full-toned sound formation. This is because you are led through a regular movement if you follow the sequence of the sounds. We will disregard the r for the moment. B – lips, s – teeth, n – tongue, g – palate, and then back from the palate to the tongue – t, n – remain for a while on the tongue, t – the same, and *sass* on the teeth. In short, if we follow the stream of sound the rule is always to make our way from the front to the back, from the back to the front, so that you do not have to jump about. You go with the sounds in succession, and because of this it is easily spoken, because you move yourself and do not jump.

Now with regard to the r, which is scattered everywhere – the labial, lingual and palatal r – it can be rolled everywhere, but one learns how to speak it best actually in context. The r's are here so that you have the opportunity of encountering them as palatal, labial or lingual sounds. You can become conscious of this in such exercises. In them you learn to understand how the sounds sit.

Labial sounds: b p m w*
Dental sounds: f* v* s s(c)h z c
Lingual sounds: n d t l
Palatal sounds: g k ch (as in loch) and ng

This last sound is present in German even if it is not counted. It is not right to separate n from g and to say *sin – gen*, but say them together, half n and half g.

*

It is good to view everything from various aspects. It can happen, for example, in everyday life that someone gives a man a photograph of his own brother and he does not recognize him. It was a profile photograph and he was used to seeing his brother full-face. One-sidedness is always harmful. It is necessary to consider all aspects, especially if you are learning to form speech.

Consider the A (ah). A child can do it. He opens his mouth wide and sends the stream of speech through it. He enjoys doing it.

The sound A (ah) is the least configurated. With the U (oo) on the other hand it is necessary to point the lips and not only form the sound plastically but configurate it to the highest degree. The other vowels lie in between. If you modify the simple procedure of A (ah), closing it more together, you get E (eh), and still more together I (ee); and if, with the aid of your lips, you make a circle, O (oh). However you do not need to point your lips until you get to U (oo).

A E I O U (ah, eh, ee, oh, oo)

Here you have really sculptural activity. The sound I (ee) lies in the middle and has the most labile balance.

---

* In the 18th lecture of the *Speech and Drama Course* (Anthroposophical Publishing Company, London, 1960) the different working together of the lower lip and upper teeth is indicated for these sounds.

*

It is equally good to learn to know the consonants from different aspects. They can also be grouped in different ways. Let us consider first the breath or 'blown' sounds. The genius of language differentiates between the various sounds. You say ef and es for f and s, but never ek and eg for k and g. Why? Because people are used through the genius of language to pronounce the breath sounds in such a way that they first voice them and then 'blow'.

Besides breath sounds we also have sounds of impact. We hit against them. In this connection you can make some very interesting studies. For example the Germans say ef – f, the Greeks say Phi – φ. In Greece it was an impact sound. In German it has become a breath sound. It is connected with the national character that in the transition from Greek to German certain impact sounds have become breath sounds.

We should get away from the habit of making the h rigid. It lies within every vowel and accompanies it.

Again, we should not say *ce-ha* (cee aitch) for ch but *ach*, for it is a breath sound.

Es(c)h – s(c)h is also a breath sound and should not be called *es-ce-ha*. It is surprising that there is no mispronunciation of es – s. It would also be better to say ev than vee – v.

Genuine impact sounds are d – de, t – te, g – ge, k – ka; but instead of en – n it should be ny or ne; instead of em – m, me or mi.

It is especially important to treat ng in German as an impact sound.

Two other kinds of sound that have a different character are:

r, a vibrating sound and
l, an undulating sound.

Functionally l is an undulating sound. Only the tongue can

undulate. The vibrating sound r is to be found everywhere except in the dental zone.

*

The following exercises serve to illustrate what has been stated above.

Without stumbling say these words, which contain all the breath sounds:

Ach, forsche rasch;   Ha, forceful rush
Es schoss so scharf   this showers as chaff
auf Schussweise   from thresher's flail

For impact sounds:

Drück die Dinge,   Tricked deep dingle
die beiden Narrenkappen   deep biting narrow copper
Tag um Tag   Dark too dark

A different version:

Tritt die Dinge, die beiden Narrenkappen Tag um Tag

Now that the significance of the individual sounds has been discussed with regard to reciting and declaiming, I would like to point out that for the epic style it is necessary to speak as pictorially as possible. The epic and lyric styles are diametrically opposed to each other. The lyric is more musical, the epic more sculptural. In the lyric style everything depends on bringing the will into action in the breath, through the feeling. The lyric style arises from deep down within the human being, even though the reciter may need to use high tones. It arises through bringing the strong activity of the will into the outgoing breath. Of the epic style it must be said that it is a striving to form – through what is spoken – the spaces, the pauses and in a wider sense actually to form the inhalation. One must develop a feeling for when it is necessary to become still and quiet between words, in order to give form to the silence.

So that the lyric style must be borne by the stream, whilst with the epic style on the contrary, one must observe moderations. This is brought about, if it is correctly understood, by using the inhalation as a pause. These two are opposites, but you will be able to give them form in this way quite naturally if you keep to what I said previously about the sounds, and to what I have just said: above all bring the sound formation to the pictorial in the epic style.

A great deal can be learnt when the sound formation is as in Uhland's *Des Sängers Fluch* (The Singer's Curse).

> *Es stand in alten Zeiten ein Schloss, so hoch und hehr,*
> *Weit glänzt es über die Lande bis an das blaue Meer.*
>
> There stood in olden times a castle so great and noble,
> Its splendour shone far over the land to the blue sea.

You will only succeed in the epic style when you paint in sounds and form the pauses in the right way.

This painting style emerges only if '*stand*' stands by itself, if A (ah) is made the most of, and the picture of standing *in alten Zeiten* has an effect of its own, becomes fixed.

Ein Schloss	try to make good use of the O (oh) so as to round off the castle.
hoch und hehr	the description follows here: its greatness and how it makes an impression
weit glänzt es	enclosed; *hoch und hehr* is interpreted in this
über die Lande	again something on its own

In this way you will have to give shape to the structuring, so that through sound formation pictures arise.

*

There are some poets who bring lyric close to the epic. This is often the case with Goethe, and Martin Greif brings it to a fine art.

An example:

Über allen Gipfeln	Over all the mountain peaks
Ist Ruh,	Is peace
In allen Wipfeln	In all the tree-tops
Spürest du	You can trace
Kaum einen Hauch;	Hardly a breath.
Die Vögelein schweigen im Walde.	The birds are silent in the wood.
Warte nur, balde	Only wait, soon
Ruhest du auch.	You will also rest.

Only right at the end do you see the introduction of emotion. In the epic retention of measure you have at first almost a pure description, from *Über allen Gipfeln* to *im Walde*, and then the lyrical ending:

> *Warte nur, balde*
> *Ruhest du auch.*

If you want to feel how you should say it, you must realize that you need your head for the first lines, the chest, and indeed the whole human being for the closing lines. In these last lines the pauses must be formed in such a way that what is said points towards the pauses and then finally the syllables themselves are filled with power.

What needs to be considered in the epic style is recitation, the element of measure. In the lyric style it is declamation, and there it is a matter of distinguishing, in a corresponding way, between high and low tone.

If you want to accustom yourself to getting the epic style completely under your control gradually, you can practise single words that have an inner plastic character:

> *Otto, tot, Anna, Ehe, Elle, Retter, Esse, Renner*
> Dead, tot, Bob, pop, cook, Anna, oboe

words that when spoken with the whole speech apparatus are capable of becoming sculptural because they can be spoken in the same way backwards.

The fact that this is so must be brought to consciousness, but the organs of speech feel it, feel that the words form themselves sculpturally in this way. Such round words – they are globular – are good to practise.

You will benefit a great deal if you frequently make your tongue say plastically a long 'globular' word such as

Reliefpfeiler   Relief-feeler

or the following globular sentences:

Ein Ledergurt trug Redel nie
Ein Neger mit Gazelle zagt im Regen nie

Did Hannah see bees? Hannah did
Take my cab back I'm Kate
Madam I'm Adam

It is exceptionally good training for the tongue to say such things for the rounding of speech. There is good reason for training the tongue through words such as these, for they round themselves off. It is good to cultivate the epic style in this way, if recitation is to be resonant and is to ring true.

Then it is good for the epic style if you try to think of words in a circle:

Fröhlich verlasse uns	Freely forsake us
Verlasse fröhlich uns	forsake us freely
Uns verlasse fröhlich	us freely forsake

One after another; in a circle, clockwise and then backwards.

⁎

Thus there are various forms of presentation: epic, lyric and dramatic. Bear in mind that in epic presentation the word is quite different from that in lyric and dramatic. In epic the word is there to portray. The listener must gain a picture from what is told. This should be achieved through the spirit of language, so the spirit of language must work too. It can only do this if the words become pictures, pictures formed through speech. Just as

93

pictures painted in space are not three-dimensional, neither does the epic presentation have the third soul-dimension. This third dimension of soul is the will. We do not make use of it in epic and can therefore apply it for portrayal, for it is indeed within us. These are the basic requirements for a speaking in the epic style.

✱

RUDOLF STEINER

COURSE ON THE ART OF SPEECH FORMATION 1922

PART II

RECORDED BY MARIE STEINER

1. Epic – the word is there to portray; the third soul-dimension must needs be lacking – the *will*. For that reason the will, that means rise and fall, can be used for description – one can make speech sculptural. *Measure*: Recitation.

2. Lyric – the word is there for the out-streaming of feeling. The third soul-dimension, the will, must needs be in it. That means one must make speech musical. *Height*: Declamation.

3. Dramatic – musically sculptural. So, if the speaker has something of his own to express – *declamation*; if he has nothing of his own to express – *recitation*.

> Naive: recitation, high
> Sentimental: declamation, low
> Character: recitation, low
> Hero: declamation, high.

Everything depends on one's drawing out of man in the widest sense that which is an artistic formation of speech in reciting and declaiming. The significance of forming the sounds of speech has already been made clear. If we would move toward a real speaking of epic and lyric we must approach the real being of man. There one must know that all speaking takes place between the breath and the movement of the blood. The measure is given by the pulse of the blood's circulation beating steadily four times during the taking of one breath. 18 breaths are equal to 72 beats. In normal speech one breath corresponds exactly to four pulse beats. That gives, moreover, a distribution of vowels and consonants. In normal speech there are four times as many consonants as vowels. In a certain sense one would speak most naturally, most precisely, if attention were paid to the relationship of the vowels to the consonants, so that for each vowel there would be four consonants.

Now, that is naturally not the case with every word; words acquire their shades of feeling just because this is not the case.

If you speak the word *Groll* (grudge) you have a word that is spoken most precisely through its sound-formation. This is made possible through the doubling of the l. With most words one stresses the breathing and for that reason the words most suitable to speech are those which contain a vowel and three consonants: *Wurm* (worm), *Mensch* (man). You can observe when you have only two consonants in a monosyllabic word how you draw this word out of itself towards the breath. This gives the different languages their special character. In a language that works strongly through the consonants, everything is brought through the language itself towards the blood. In a language that works through the vowels everything is drawn towards the breath and thereby towards reflection. Insight into this is only one of the bases for dramatic speaking, which must arise out of the situation itself.

If I try to emphasize the vowels and, in so doing, speak slowly, I turn toward the breath. If I emphasize the consonants and speak quickly, I turn toward the blood. Notice the very fine nuances you can produce in dramatic speaking when you pay attention to such things. You will generally speak what is reflective slowly, thereby bringing out the vowels. You will speak what is emotive rapidly, thereby stressing the consonants.

It might also occur that the general rule is reversed if a person is quite beside himself. Thoughts are generally expressed slowly, stressing the vowels, but if I want to indicate that he who speaks suffers from a kind of flightiness in the realm of ideas, is beside himself, so that it is not he who has the thoughts but the thoughts that have him, I must go over to stressing the consonants and speaking rapidly. The audience is naive. It hears what is in keeping with nature. For that reason he who fantasizes in a slow tempo on the stage will never satisfy – only he who gives vent to fantasy rapidly.

The opposite is the case however when the will comes into the picture, excitement. As long as I speak as a fairly healthy person I must stress the consonants: if I am half dead, like Attinghausen, I must stress the vowels and speak slowly, for the naive listener experiences it in the way I have described. If you have a fellow who has experienced something intensely and he comes to tell you about it, it is not reflection on what he has to report that is preponderant but the wish to impart it. In that case he must use the consonants and speak quickly. It must be clear that he who listens is in the opposite mood, even if he has been shattered. He needs time for reflection in order to grasp the matter in the first place, so he will speak slowly to begin with, using the vowels. And a specially dramatic effect is achieved if the listener goes over from speaking slowly and vocalically, to speaking rapidly and consonantally. He thereby shows through speech formation that he is interested and understands. This on the other hand puts a damper on the excitement of the messenger who has arrived. He calms down and goes over into speaking slowly and vocalically and therewith, if you observe this, you have dramatic dialogue in speech formation. You can find aspects in this which will be fruitful for the treatment of dialogue.

Let us take the scene that precedes William Tell's monologue. It is a question of studying the scene in such a way that one always tries to find out what nuances are to be given. For that reason I shall call a preliminary rehearsal in order to indicate the various nuances required. The director must make an effort to seek out contrasting characters. For instance: Walter Fürst, Stauffacher and Baumgarten – these are people who do not go beyond a certain degree of enthusiasm, who contain their enthusiasm. The calmest is Stauffacher. Baumgarten is somewhat more fiery, and Fürst is honest. Hedwig is very emotional. Attinghausen must be shown to be dying. Rudenz must be played in such a way that one at least sees through his egotism and his tendency to speak in clichés. Melchtal is fieriest of all who believes to his innermost core what he has to say. This is the preliminary preparation for the Tell monologue.

Now I would like to draw your attention to a kind of nuancing in reading. It is not yet so clearly worked out as when it is acted, but it is necessary to show to begin with how the threads must run and then to rise to a climax at the end of the scene, before the monologue.

Tell: calm, until '*Mach deine Rechnung . . .*'
               '*Zum Ungeheuren hast du mich gewöhnt*' – long pause.
               '*Die armen Kindlein*' – restrained; gradually becoming furious.

*

Hedwig:*   not only towards emotional heights but also emotional depths
Attinghausen: gradually getting faster, but fading away.
Rudenz: must try to take the vowels more fully, because otherwise the voice gets lost in space.
Melchtal: the l's do not come out yet; they trickle instead of streaming out.

* The scenes (Act IV, Scenes 2 and 3) were read by Rudolf Steiner and those taking part in the course. Then Rudolf Steiner made the following comments.

99

Tell: good. – '*Auf dieser Bark von Stein . . .*' that was not yet thoroughly felt. Then: '*Ich laure auf ein edles Wild*' – a slight shade of irony, which must be achieved by a duller and shorter E (eh). You must always have some idea of the stage business to be done and therefore the pauses were too short.

This can perhaps show you how you can endeavour to give form to speech. With Attinghausen hold on really firmly so that at the end he speaks rather fast but allows it to fade away.

*

Reciting makes the same kind of demands as playing the piano. To begin with you must know the rules, then they must become second nature so that the listener does not notice that rules are being applied. By applying the rules, by introducing as much variation as possible, you give the true impression of being natural. This is the case in every art.

One must always be conscious of the fact that the fourth wall is missing, that one sees life in relief. Style is connected with this. For this reason you may not speak merely naturalistically and for this reason also you must find positions that are suitable to the relief. It is impossible to want to be naturalistic on the stage. You must find positions at most in quarter profile. The achievement of this is the art of direction. Whilst speaking you cannot turn your back on the audience. The stage must simply be regarded as a picture of life in relief.

Then you must notice that all consonants are harder to understand in large halls than in small, if they are not sufficiently supported by vowels. Special attention must be paid to this.

The dramatic is actually a synthesis, a combination of lyric and epic, supported naturally through mime in spontaneous portrayal.

Let us assume that you recognize in a dramatic piece that someone wants to convey something with enthusiasm. In that case you must look to the consonants and let the vowels fall away. You must speak the consonants with emphasis, then you evoke in the audience through speech formation the impression of someone imparting something with enthusiasm. So: allow the vowels to fall away, stress the consonants, and avoid a slow tempo.

Let us now assume we have to communicate something of a contemplative nature. The listener should have the impression: that is a thoughtful person; he makes us aware of something. In that case it is necessary to stress the vowels, to let the consonants fall away, and to speak slowly. You achieve in this way what has to be achieved simply through your treatment of speech. By realizing the value of such things you can create the right kind of transition. Let us assume that someone communicates something and notices that someone else listens intently. He can then go over from the fast consonantal way of speaking to the slower vocalic way. So at first he was enthusiastic; he noticed he was not being understood; he wants to convince; he goes over to a slower tempo. – This introduces shading and nuance. Or a contemplative person says something; he notices the other person does not understand him; he is quiet for a moment; then goes over from a slow to a quick tempo. What the onlooker is to feel must be achieved through the emotion and the image of speech. In this way you will see what it is to be understood as speech formation. Those who recite and declaim ought not to be so importunate as to want to work through their own life of feeling. That belongs to the process of preparation. When you recite you must have that behind you and work through speech formation.

There are not many good directors these days – just Reinhardts – and not many good speakers – just Moissis. If the stage had four walls one could direct like Reinhardt. Otherwise if one directs in such a way, one is simply making believe for oneself and the audience. In painting, colour and light and shade are not the only material. There is the surface, and one must experience in the surface. The pure perspective of space is basically something sculptural. You have nothing original when you paint a perspective in space but you have something plastic.

Painting must reckon with the surface, the stage with three walls. It is necessary to be aware that the stage and the audience constitute a whole. It is not possible to leave the audience out of account. Those who have a feeling for the totality of the thing in hand will ask themselves: What does it mean if I allow the actor to come forward from the back? This is something that belongs to the artistic medium. It is not possible to make arbitrary movements on the stage any more than it is possible to make blobs arbitrarily on a canvas.

Take an example. Somebody comes from the back of the stage to the front. This means that he is now saying something of an intimate character. The listener on the stage must already be in front; the other must take a few steps forward, then the character of intimacy comes out. But how does the characteristic of speaking to a number of people come to expression? Imagine that someone wants to say something to a group, that is publicly. He stands there, then starts to go backwards with a gesture that more or less expresses: Children, I want to tell you something!

These are things that must stand before the imagination when it comes to stage direction. One must know about technique, but in a human way.

And now to continue – if you have someone who has something to say that arouses interest he will have to go from left to right, never from right to left. If you have a passage that you know must impress, must arouse understanding, but not emotional interest, you must go from right to left. This is because the left eye has more of a soul nature and the right more of an intellectual nature.

Such things belong of necessity to the true creation of a scene and to the formation of the dramatic element in the right way out of fantasy. The dramatic element must be placed within the whole situation. Naturalism has merely cultivated dilettantism. Art is something different from the merely natural in the sense-world. For that reason you must only with your gestures do what is essential. In plays seen nowadays characters are continually lighting cigarettes because they have no feeling for anything but an imitation of what happens in everyday life. But everything depends on creating something artistic. If a young boy, for instance, lights a cigarette, it can give a certain nuance. It can characterize, but if old people do it we learn nothing about their character, as we do with the youngster. It might be that the boy lights cigarettes, and in the next act one looks for him. He is not there. Light is cast on the progress of the play. So it should be a rule to do only what is necessary in the course of the play.

You will have seen that for recitation and declamation everything depends on experiencing speech, word and sound. The element of death has worked so long on human culture that we must regard it as our earnest task to introduce the element of life. Experiencing the sound, though, is not as easy as you might perhaps think. Let us assume you want to experience through your feeling a noise of some kind, and then let it flow through your speech. What do you find nowadays in the way of theories about the origin of speech? There are two theories – the so-called ding-dong theory and the so-called bow-wow theory.

The ding-dong theory assumes that language speaks to us in the manner of bells; speech is a mysterious imitation of the inorganic, whilst the bow-wow theory assumes that language is a further development in the human realm of sounds existing in the animal world. Not much has come of these theories in the realm of the handling of speech, for they move at an intellectual level. The truth is that language moves at an emotional level and can be understood only through spiritual knowledge.

*

Krik krak kruk   crick crack crook ·

This is a useful exercise for rendering passages in poems in which you have the same expression of feeling as in *krak* or *krik* or *kruk*. In monologues you can tell whether you experience them in the *krak* or *krik* or *kruk* mood.

Kr – noise

Krak: something sudden: crashing noise
Kruk: something continuous and loud
You will be able to recite the part of a herald in roughly the right way after a preparatory exercise of this kind.
Krik – mood: sharply penetrating. Use this if you want to bring to expression something you wish to make quite clear, in the manner of a pedantic schoolmaster, for instance.
Krak: Mephistopheles in *Faust*, Prologue in Heaven: *Da du, O Herr, dich einmal wieder nahst...*
Krik: Wagner in *Faust*, Easter promenade: *Mit euch, Herr Doktor, zu spazieren...* or *Welch ein Gefühl musst du, O grosser Mann...*
Kruk: The Lord in *Faust*, Prologue in Heaven: *Hast du mir weiter nichts zu sagen?*

Such seemingly senseless exercises are quite useful because the soul has a different form of experience each time. Particularly in our time, in which we are so abstract, it is not easy to make the experience of language our own. Who, for instance, still feels what lies in the word *Begeisterung* (enthusiasm)? *Begeisterung* has the word *Geist* (thous or theos) in it. That the divine Spirit flashes through us is considered by no one. The genius of language does not speak to man these days.

An infinite wealth of life is expressed through the fact that we have *schön* (beautiful), *hässlich* (ugly) as polar opposites. *Schein* (appearance) is what flows through the world. It becomes fixed, somewhat opaque. If the *Schein* is held fast: *Schön.*

What withholds its being, does not show itself to me, I hate. *hass ich*: *hässlich* (ugly). There you have the contrast.

When I speak of something beautiful, I love its appearance, I can describe it objectively. Hideousness hides itself from me. I cannot describe it objectively so I remain subjective.

We cannot begin to approach the art of recitation without entering into language in such a way that the words start to say something to us.

*

The genius of language has a cosmic conscience. It bore witness to this in those ages in which one could hear the spirit of language.

Take as an example: m – z – g

You know a labial sound is   m   *Mund* (mouth)

a dental sound is   z   *Zahn* (tooth)

a palatal sound is   g   *Gaumen* (palate)

Even when the genius of language makes jokes it does so correctly: *Maul* (mouth).

It should not be fixed in abstract formulae because that would miss the point.

For instance: w is a soft consonant. This is clearly seen in the following exercise:

> *Weiche wehendem Winde auf Wiesenwegen*
> Wider wavering winds fan weaving ways

We only have consonants here that feel at home in the w. All consonants are houses of the zodiac; all vowels houses of the planets. But if anyone makes a theory out of it I shall ask of him: have you never heard the word *Wucht* (force)? There the w is not in its own house. The nature of the w is overcome. The soft nature of the w is hardened.

Wuchtig	*wogt*	*Wirbelwind*
Weightily	waved	whirlwind

You must find your way through practice into the varying moods, and not just theorize.

> *Du zweifelst, du zürnest, du zerreissest zornig*
> Thou scarest, thou scornest, thou scoldest scoffing

You have painted with the sounds what occurs. You will always find a destructive element in the z. In passages such as this, which are torn and rent, throw the z at the head of the listener. Feel concretely the difference between this and the following:

Zweifle nicht, zürne nicht, zerreisse nicht zornig
Scarest not, scornest not, scoldest not scoffing

So one can create the possibility of pouring gentleness over what speech does. It can have a very beautiful effect when its original meaning is overcome by what the soul reclaims from it.

Consider how you gradually find your way into the s in the sentence:

Sieh silberne Segel auf fliessendem Wasser
See silvery sails on fleecy waves

and how, with your speech, you follow a complete path when you say:

Rauschende Reden rollten im Raume
Rushing phrases roll around the room

Let us assume someone has been to a meeting and wants to express briefly what occurred. There were several speakers, all of whom were acceptable and spoke well. The whole event was stimulating. He wants to bring to consciousness that (a) there was content, (b) it had a lasting effect (c) he was somewhere where it happened.

We want to bring five shades of meaning into the sentence. We have an impression on the senses to begin

with in:	*Rauschende*
then the thought element:	*Reden*
the impression in the realm of emotion:	*rollten*
the rolling starts to coagulate (like an egg-shell):	*Raume*

So it is given such shades of meaning as can only be given by sensing the sounds themselves.

The study of speech itself will lead you best along the right lines.

Notice how the impression of something granular lies in such words as:

Grau Gries Granat Graupe   Grey gritty granite grounds

and how you yourself must feel grittiness when you say:

Greulich ist das   gruesome are they

Let us assume you want to feel all that lies in spr. You can feel it best if you go with your speaking from behind forwards. For instance with such words as:

Sprache	open your mouth
Sprechen	close it a little
Spritzen	close it still more
Sprossen	come forward to your lips
Sprudeln	then point your lips

These things all have some kinship as regards sound, although they have different meanings.

You ought also to try and practise the positions of the consonantal relationships, in that you observe the various pitches in:

Bim bam bum   Bim bam boom

It is good to practise running upstairs, as it were, with such words as:

Schl – *Schlüpfrig schlemmen schlicken*   Slippery slimy slinker
Gl – *Glas gleich glotzen*   Glass glide glottis

Think of the fine differentiations in:

Flaum Flocke Flamme   Flounce flocks flaming

In this way you combine the movements of speech so that you

speak the sounds correctly in a given word. The unconscious genius of speech must do a great deal but you yourself must prepare through exercises such as these if you wish to recite properly.

*

Yesterday I read a passage from *William Tell* where Schiller portrays something characteristic, something individual and human. Schiller succeeds in doing this also in *The Bride of Messina*, where he is concerned with the aesthetic element. In the chorus we have the echo of the experience of what is said. We have something aesthetic here.

I would like to draw your attention to the way Schiller prepares the dialogue between Don Cesar and Don Manuel by giving different forms to the aesthetic aspect. What kind of person is Don Cesar? Hot-blooded. He speaks with passion. So I would make him speak quickly and consonantally. Don Manuel, by way of contrast, is the thoughtful one; so I would make him speak slowly, stressing the vowels.

I want to present this in a production. It would not occur to me to put Don Cesar into a blue costume or Manuel into a red one. I would do the opposite: I shall dress Cesar, because he is in the process of cooling down, in yellow; Manuel, because he must hold out, in blue-green (blue would be too restraining).

Cesar's words are reddish-yellow
Manuel's words are blue-green

Schiller prepares the way for this by allowing the dramatic element to be half lyric in the character of Isabella. She is out to win the people. We shall only strike the right note in the chorus if we bring it into a certain sphere of universality. It could come from the air; it has something elemental and spirit-like out of which at particular moments the single speaker must step forward.

Isabella is in deep mourning, hence dark; so also are her words.*

The poet is in such a situation here that he cannot do other than shape the speech consonantally. Alexander Strakosch, the well-known speech teacher and artist, when asked for his advice used to say: 'More feeling, feeling'. It was not possible for him to feel his way into the sounds; it was not possible for him to escape from the abstract into the concrete, but he was a dear person. Once when everyone was talking about Hamlet and giving their opinions about the famous monologue, Strakosch, when asked for his opinion, replied: 'Very inward.'

In order to experience the beauties of the *Bride of Messina* you must have the key to the work. You will not be able to approach it with the superficial way of speaking that is usual nowadays, but you will have to enter into the plastic element.

Dialogue between Isabella and Diego.
The emotional element has always to do with consonants and gets quicker.
Now the element of observation.
Now the chorus: recitation entirely; every trace of declamation must go. First chorus: *Dich begrüsse ich in Ehrfurcht.*
One might think the first chorus ought to be taken at a low pitch and the second high, but speech formation produces the opposite.
Second chorus: *Mögen sie's wissen . . .*, low, emotional.
A speaker from the first chorus. *Und jetzt sehen wir uns als Knechte, untertan diesem fremden Geschlechte!* Highly emotional.
A second speaker from the first chorus: *Wohl! Wir bewohnen ein glückliches Land . . .* The mood of thoughtfulness is shot through with emotion. Hence both vowels and consonants, but the vowels should be preponderant.

*

There is a poem that describes what splendid heroes there

* Act I, Scenes 1–3.

were in southern Russia at certain times in the Middle Ages. In prose one would simply relate that they are there and would give their names. In poetry the effect is attained in the following way:

> No one surpasses Ilya in ingenuity.
> No one surpasses Dobrinya in giant strength.
> No one surpasses Marko in daring.
> No one surpasses Podok in beauty.
> No one surpasses Igor in courtesy.
> No one surpasses Yaroslav in rhetoric.
> No one surpasses Vladimir in mightiness.
> No one surpasses Nikita in gracefulness.

You must enter into the structure of the lines in such a way that the listener enjoys listening while you enumerate a number of attributes. It will be acceptable to the listener if you speak these words with especially rounded contours. You see here how the words 'no one' are repeated eight times; the foreign names are of no interest to the listener. One's task is to concentrate on throwing into relief through speech formation those features which hold the attention of the audience. The listener is so interested in those features that it is refreshing for him to hear in between the words that mean nothing to him. The listener is not prevented by things of no importance from grasping what is the main thing for him.

Through your preparation you must always take care that nothing is lost to the listener. You must achieve a great deal through pauses or by giving speech configuration, letting certain things fall and throwing others into relief.

You will keep contact with your listener if, in such a period, you give shape to speech in a way that works out what lies within it by bringing out its special qualities. You must take care of this and for this reason cultivate the attribute of being your own audience. In preparation bring it to the point that others will listen to you later because you have listened to yourself when alone.

Recitation has degenerated to such an extent that it is difficult for people nowadays to even guess it is an art.

Speech arose out of fantasy. It preceded the development of the intellect. The cancer of our age is that there are so many clever people nowadays and so few artists. Art is connected with joy. You must derive pleasure from speaking. There is no such thing as words that are ugly in themselves. If you try to discover the beauty of speech you will have plenty to do and you will derive pleasure from it.

*

Those taking part in the course speak the exercises:

Lalle Lieder lieblich . . .   Lulling leader limply . . .

Rudolf Steiner makes the following remarks:

Notice how each consonant becomes plastic when one feels how it is made to move differently through its neighbouring vowels. –

Try to bring the sound up out of the lungs; in the production of sound you must take note of what lies above; what lies below serves to provide the air, which then creates the sound in front. –

Your voice is strong but your voice is not sufficiently mobile; there is mucus sounding too. –

Only if you shift the tone forward will you get the sounds plastic. –

The sound still strikes against your tongue; it must be brought more to the front. –

Your voice is not yet in the sound. –

Good. But there is still something there which does not free the space between the sounds. –

You still hold too strongly to the thought and do not go into the sound. –

The impression of the poem must be acquired through sound-formation, not through thought. But if you demand the latter it would be as if a statue were moving towards the observer. –

Still too much thrusting. You must accustom yourself to making rounded sounds just as one makes rounded movements in eurythmy. –

It only slips into the declamatory element after having been assimilated, when one no longer needs to think of the content. –

When you learn a poem by heart you will only have a kind of substitute for what you have to recite. –

Only that can be shaped as a work of art which has entered into the soul, and crept into it as a matter of course, through reflection, through living with it in sympathy. Something can help you to become clear about this. Try to bring what you learnt twenty years ago into the tone. That gives an experience through which more is learnt than through theoretical instruction. –

Do the exercise more slowly, so that the l can be given shape. The sound still sits in your nose. –

There is a raw-sounding resonance; in such a case it helps if you do little recitation exercises after you have sucked a lump of sugar. –

The tone sits too far back in the head. –

Good material. You will achieve a great deal if you get used to slipping into the sound. –

In the onward flow of your sound there is still something that has the effect of a cord; it must be modelled, moulded. –

The last remark would also apply here; only there is still a singing sound in the nose. –

The sound lies too far back, not far enough forward. –

The tone is too sharp; one could try to practise something from one of Ahriman's scenes, where there is an opportunity of driving the sound into the cheeks.*–

The sound needs more depth; it is like a resonance in the

---

* The remark refers to Ahriman, a figure in Rudolf Steiner's Mystery Plays (Steiner Book Centre, Toronto, 1973), Rudolf Steiner gave a special indication about the 'pocket-in-the-cheek' for the forming of speech in this role.

right nostril . . . Too much nasal resonance leads to one-sidedness. –

You must learn to modulate the sound more, the way in which an A (ah) and an O (oh) is studied. –

Well yes, that must be rescued from decadence; you must take possession of the tone instead of simply blasting it out. –

The story of Demosthenes must really be taken seriously. Everything depends on facing the obstacles one has oneself created. –

The voice places itself when it is brought into the right position. For instance, in the exercise: *Sende aufwärts* . . . (Send thou upwards . . .) imagine that your tongue has to become a kind of boat through all six lines. –

Difficulties in the breath exercise: *Erfüllung geht* . . . (Fulfilling goes . . .)

It is a help if you reverse the words; for instance, *wollen –nellow.* Also reverse the words that have double consonants or double vowels: *Seele – Elees.* –

Speak words forwards and backwards: *Eva – Ave.* The inward nature lying in *Ave* comes of itself if you practise it in reverse as *Eva.* –

The passing over from thought to sound must become a matter of experience. –

*

Those taking part in the course say, one after the other, the breath exercise:

> *In den unermesslich weiten Räumen . . .*
> In the vast unmeasured world-wide spaces . . .

Rudolf Steiner comments:

Penetrate into the sound. Take your own tone along with you to begin with so that everything rings and vibrates in sympathy. –

Then the exercises:

Sturm-Wort rumort um Tor und Turm . . . Storm wolf roars forth
. . . and *Ei ist weisslich* . . . Eye is viceless . . .
It must be rounded off. The consonants are trapped in the
physical organism. –
The nasal membranes are sounding here as well. –
Get rid of the tremolo. –
It will do; it needs practise. –
Still more tone. –
The resonance has a tremolo, –
Watch your breath. –
A bit more practise. –
Good. –
The voice is a little pinched in the middle; it must get broader. –
A little bit high; not bad. –
Put more into the sounds. –
You will gain a lot if you try to make the denser sounds more
flexible as your speech is not yet articulated. –
That will do. –
Will also be good, if practised often. –
Go really slowly; get used to the slower effect through slower
speaking. –
Bring it away from the nose. –
You must damp it down a little. –
Try to let the air strike the back of the palate. –
A fuller tone. –
Watch the difference between *ei* – *Blei* – in the mouth and *ai* –
Maid – further back.–
Get used to a brighter ai for ai. –

✻

Those taking part in the course speak the exercises:

Mäuse messen mein Essen   Moisten mason mine essence

Lämmer leisten leises Läuten   Lamer lightness Liza loiters

Bei biedern Bauern bleib brav   By beaten bowers bide brave

Komm kurzer kräftiger Kerl   Come crooked craftiest cur´

You must get away from the A (ah) mood. You modify every vowel with it. Practise exercises that have no A (ah). That is what prevents people from entering into it. A (ah) is the sound that makes other people aware of your being there. In b on the other hand lies the sheltering of oneself: I am inside my house. This is all in the exercise: *Abracadabra*. –
I would advise you, if you want to bring it out, to press on the tip of your nose, then you will get the roundness you need. –
I advise you to practise an exercise slowly, sometimes making a spitting movement between the syllables. –
Your voice could be developed, but you must press your cheeks together when practising. –
The following exercise will help you: *Bei biedern Bauern bleib brav*. By beaten bowers bide brave. –
For you the following exercises alternately: *Lämmer leisten leises Läuten* Lamer lightness Liza loiters *Komm kurzer kräftiger Kerl* Come crooked craftiest cur. –
For you: *Mäuse messen mein Essen* Moisten mason mine essence. *Komm kurzer kräftiger Kerl*. Come crooked craftiest cur. –
I would advise you to speak the four exercises as far as possible with gestures, to gain power. –
Here the first three exercises are useful, the last less so. You must practise the O (oh), because you say o -oo.
Lämmer leisten leises Läuten Lamer lightness Liza loiters *Komm kurzer kräftiger Kerl* Come crooked craftiest cur alternately. I would advise you to practise while stepping. –
Here the voice must be taken back from the lips. –
You must lay yourself into the sound, weave in it. –
You must try to take your voice back and practise with your hands in your trouser pockets. –
A little artificial. You are not quite in it. You must get down into it. –
Your voice is not bad but the pitch is too high. –
The l exercise. –

Mainly the b exercise. –

The k exercise would be beneficial to you. –

*

You must still do the exercise: *Dumm tobt Wurm-Molch* . . . Doom
taught wolves bold . . . An A (ah) is still sounding through it. –

The light exercise: *Ei is weisslich* . . . Eye is viceless . . . An U (oo)
is sounding through it. –

In the fable of the horse and the bull say the horse's last words at
the back of your tongue, not at the front. –

In the fable of the nightingale and the peacock you mustn't rob
yourself of the possibility of intensification, which you do if
you start so loudly. –

Better, because gradation is possible. It is articulated but you
must control your voice more and not let it run along on its
own. –

It is essential to eradicate the slight singing. –

*

Additional remark: Some people emit an eh-eh-eh after every
third word. They are constipated. A person who is more fluid in
body does not recite like one who is constipated. You cannot
tackle this medically but you can achieve everything if you start
off from the sounds.

*

Those taking part in the course practise the 6th and the 9th
scenes from Rudolf Steiner's Mystery Play: *The Soul's Probation*.

The peasants are characterized only through their speech
formation.

1st Man:	Has to do with I (ee).
2nd Man:	E (eh), r. – Go into the sound: must become accustomed to deft speaking through lip exercises and must become more plastic.

116

1st Woman:	E (eh), r. The same. She wants to say something to the others which she thinks she alone knows.
3rd Man:	Palate sounds are all-important.
2nd Woman:	Articulate the consonants strongly.
3rd Woman:	Prepare for the consonants with m.
4th Man:	A liberal fellow, tuned to E (eh) and I (ee); rather a loud gentleman.
5th Man:	A visionary: U (oo), O (oh).
4th Woman:	Pseudo piety, dependent on the E (eh), a bit hypocritical.
5th Woman:	I (ee); revolutionary in tone.
6th Woman:	Increased piety; tune in to the diphthongs and adjust the rest accordingly: speak more inwardly.
6th Man:	Clever prattler, crafty; try particularly to use the broad E (eh). Then you bring out through speech formation, through a broad E (eh), the untrue, slightly hypocritical element.
Jew:	Should have nothing naturalistic but something of a singing quality in his speech. S exercise as preparation.
Monk:	Good. If it were taken with a more hollow voice it would then be properly graded.

*

Bertha:	Really naive but not sentimental.
Joseph Kühne:	He is too indifferent, too disinterested; not sufficiently penetrating.
Frau Kühne:	Too epic; not sufficiently dramatic.
1st and 2nd Men:	Bring more life into it.
3rd Woman:	If you think your way into the scene you will speak more out of the situation.
Monk:	The monologue shows why the monk is not understood by Reinecke: there is a change in him.

*

Scene 8 of the *Guardian of the Threshold* is read. It is the scene with six townsmen and six townswomen. Rudolf Steiner remarks: The naming of the people already gives an indication of what they are like.

Ferdinand Reinecke (fox)　　　　Friedrich Geist (enspirited)
Michael Edelmann (nobleman)　　Caspar Stürmer (firebrand)
Bernard Redlich (upright)　　　　Georg Wahrmund (truthful)
Franziska Demut (humble)　　　　Marie Kühne (bold)
Maria Treufels (loyal)　　　　　　Hermine Hauser (provincial)
Luise Fürchtegott (God fearing)　Katharina Ratsam (prudent)

*

For the consolidation of speech:

Wäge dein Wollen klar,　　　　Clearly weigh thine acts of will
Richte dein Fühlen wahr　　　　Truthfully direct thy feelings
Stähle dein Denken starr.　　　　And thy thinking starkly steel.
Starres Denken trägt,　　　　　　Stark thinking bears thee
Rechtes Fühlen wahrt,　　　　　　Truthful feeling guards thee
Klarem Wollen folgt die Tat.　　Deeds follow clear-weighed will.

*

The shading of the three soul forces, Philia, Astrid and Luna from *The Portal of Initiation*.

Philia:
Ich will erfüllen mich　　　　　　I will imbue myself
Mit klarstem Lichtessein　　　　with clearest essence of the light
Aus Weltenweiten,　　　　　　　from world-wide spaces,
Ich will eratmen mir　　　　　　I will breathe in sound-substance
Belebenden Klangesstoff　　　　life-bestowing,
Aus Aetherfernen,　　　　　　　from far ethereal regions,
Dass dir, geliebte Schwester,　that you, beloved sister, with your
Das Werk gelingen kann.　　　　may reach your goal.　　　[work

118

Astrid:

Ich will verweben	And I will weave
Erstrahlend Licht	into the radiant light
Mit dämpfender Finsternis,	the clouding darkness.
Ich will verdichten	I will condense
Das Klangesleben.	the life of sound,
Es soll erglitzernd klingen,	that glistening it may ring
Es soll erklingend glitzern,	and ringing it may glisten,
Dass du, geliebte Schwester,	that you, beloved sister,
Die Seelenstrahlen lenken kannst.	may guide the rays of soul.

Luna:

Ich will erwärmen Seelenstoff	I will enwarm soul-substance
Und will erhärten Lebensäther.	and will make firm life-ether.
Sie sollen sich verdichten,	They shall condense themselves,
Sie sollen sich erfühlen,	they shall perceive themselves,
Und in sich selber seiend	and in themselves residing
Sich schaffend halten,	guard their creative forces,
Dass du, geliebte Schwester,	that you, beloved sister.
Der suchenden Menschenseele	within the seeking soul
Des Wissens Sicherheit erzeugen	may quicken certainty of know-
kannst.	ledge.

M	Devotion
L	Self-surrender
N	Withdrawal into oneself
R	Aggressive element
S	Destructive element
W B	Enveloping oneself

(from a notebook)

*

During the summer and autumn courses the following poems out of *Wir fanden einen Pfad* by Christian Morgenstern were also recited:

Nun wohne Du darin . . . as exercise: *Schwinge schwere Schwalbe* swinging swirling swallow
O Nacht, du Sternenbronnen . . . as O (oh) exercise
An Viele/An Manche/An Einige
Wer vom Ziel nichts weiss. . . . .
Das blosse Wollen einer grossen Güte.

119

And in addition the scene in the spirit realm from *The Portal of Initiation*, as above.

*

In conclusion I would still like to point out to you that if you want to approach speech seriously you must treat it as an art, not as a mere polishing up of everyday speech.

This attitude must fill your soul when you practise recitation and declamation. When you say something in prose people are interested in the content. Actually you must waive this in recitation, in artistic speaking, and simply see that you interest people through the 'how'. In that case you must not shrink from works that are well known. We, as humanity, have unfortunately come to the point where immense treasures of spiritual life still extant are no longer presented in public. Even in ordinary listening we analyse too much and do not enter into the experience enough as human beings. You must therefore do something about it if good art is to be preserved for humanity. Nowadays a person of twenty thinks he no longer needs to let a play such as *Iphigenia* work upon him because he has already gone through it in school. This is a great pity, because you can only draw the best from certain cultural treasures if you enjoy them over and over again. There are quite a few people nowadays who cannot tell the difference between the poems of Goethe and Geibel, although Geibel himself said that so long as there were teenagers his poems would live. The student of recitation and declamation requires a sure aesthetic judgment because he must work, albeit unconsciously, as an educator. If he reads Wildenbruch, for example, under the illusion that he is a poet, his aesthetic judgment is clouded. You need this kind of backbone in order to face criticisms that do not stem even from the public. We would be better able to judge if theatre directors were not of the opinion that they could offer inferior material to the public. If recitation and declamation are to be practised it is essential that people should allow the artistic element to influence them from many different aspects. Prose takes effect through its content. When you recite it must be clear to you that you achieve everything through speech formation.

RUDOLF STEINER

SPEECH EXERCISES
WITH EXPLANATIONS

NOVEMBER 1923

RECORDED BY MARIE STEINER

A course on the art of speech formation was held by Marie Steiner in The Hague from 13 to 18 November 1923 in connection with the founding of the Waldorf School. Rudolf Steiner gave as always his explanations in connection with the exercises. The following series of new exercises was added to those already known and published here, and these took into account the gutteral nature of the Dutch language.

We begin with an entry in a notebook dated 17 November 1923.

*

North Sea peoples: more consonants than vowels.
Avoidance of vowels prevents cold air from streaming into the
    lungs.
Mountain dwellers: palatal and throat sounds.
Flat regions: lip sounds.
Educated people: more consonants.

In order to bring the voice forward:

> *Sturm-Wort rumort um Tor und Turm*
> *Molch-Wurm bohrt durch Tor und Turm*
> *Dumm tobt Wurm-Molch durch Tor und Turm*
>
> Storm wolf roars forth through door and tomb
> Bold wolves bored through door and tomb
> Doom taught wolves bold through door and tomb.

Against the Dutch l:

> *Walle welle willig*
> The villages nestle in the valleys and the vales
>
> *Leise lispeln lumpige Lurche lustig*
> Lightly lisping lumpety lurcher lusty

Sounds of impact and breath sounds together are good for tendencies to stutter or for sluggish speech organs:

Hitzige strahlige stachelige	Hit singer startlingly shocking
Sturzstränge stützen	storms stringy shootings
Straff Netze nützlich als	stiff nets knits Stephen's sister
Stramme Tatzen streng	strumming dances
Gefalzt	strong and fast
Ist strauchelnder Stern	Hist! strategy stern
Meister mystischer Stufen?	masters mystical stages
Stell stets ernsten Strebens	stale states earnest stripling
Sternstrasse standhaft	stern stresses steadfast
Still streng stehend	still strength sheltered
Vor Stufen steten Strebens	for stooping straightened strip-lings
In ständger Stimmung.	with stridency strumming

*

Exercise for a participant, in order to bring his speech further forward. His voice was placed too far back and was lodged in his nose in the region of the soft palate, causing him to become hoarse.

Kurze knorrige knochige Knaben
Knicken manchem Männchen
Manchmal manchen Knorpel

*

Read a short poem through twice. You must make up your mind about the two kinds of delivery. One, stressing the vowels: it becomes warm; one, stressing the consonants: it becomes cold. If you want to recite with warmth you must lay the most stress on the vowels; if you want to recite with coolness you must lay the most stress on the consonants.

If you want to express the fact that an element of will lies in the nature of the thing you must take the palatal sounds. Stress these especially and then you will acquire the characteristic of manifesting an element of will:

Ganz kurze krumme Christbäume kann man kaufen
Gaunt crooked Christmas logs can men cover

But if you want to bring feeling to expression instead of hard-hitting will, then you must take the labial sounds. You sense the feeling as it were flowing on your lips:

Welche Bürde lebt im prüfenden Leben
Welfare burdens lived in proving labour

The first exercise, which is a palatal one, causes you to have a feeling in your heels. Stepping helps to produce the palatal sounds. What lives on the lips lives in the hands; What originates in the palate, in your feet.

*

Return again and again to the word already spoken, shade it differently. Through this kind of inner rhythm, that rests on repetition, find different nuances:

Weisse Helligkeit scheinet in die schwarze Finsternis
Die schwarze Finsternis ergreift die fühlende Seele
Die fühlende Seele ersehnet die weisse Helligkeit
Die weisse Helligkeit ist der wollende Seelentrieb
Der wollende Seelentrieb findet die weisse Helligkeit
In der weissen Helligkeit webet die sehnende Seele –

White clearness shines into black darkness
Black darkness grasps the feeling soul
The feeling soul longs for the white clearness
White clearness is the willing soul impulse
The willing soul impulse finds the white clearness
In the white clearness weaves the longing soul

At the end of the course they also practised:
Grenzen der Menschheit by Goethe.
Nixe Binsefuss by Mörike.

EXERCISES FOR SENSING SOUNDS

*Lechzend lernte er erst ernste Lehren**

Feel E (eh) in such a way that wherever it appears you sense a slight amazement.

Zierlich Ding ist nicht Wind nicht Wirrnis

Feel I (ee) like a bright reddish ray going in different directions.

Voll Lob zog wohl noch Gotthold fort

Feel O (oh) as if there were a surrounding of something in your feeling.

Und du musst zur Ruh

Feel U (oo) as a withdrawal of yourself in your feeling.

*

For stammerers:†

> *Leicht lief letztlich*
> *Rasch rollend rädergleich*
> *Mein Mut machtvoll*
>
> *Brause prächtig prunkend*
> *Durch das dortige Dickicht*

---

* No A (ah) exercise was found in these residual notes.
† Given for a special case where there were wrong movements in the diaphragm of which one had to be aware and which had to be corrected through practice.

MARIE STEINER

THE ART OF RECITATION

APHORISTIC REMARKS AND NOTES

FROM WORK IN THE SECTION FOR THE ARTS OF
SPEECH AND MUSIC AT THE GOETHEANUM

THE ART OF RECITATION
WITH ADDITIONS* BY RUDOLF STEINER

It simply has to be stated for the sake of style that many believe anyone can recite without training.

An extraordinarily strong interest in the art of recitation has been aroused recently in many circles. People are beginning to realize that even where there is a natural gift we are dealing with an art that can only be mastered with trouble and toil and earnestness, so that, *as in other arts*, the goddess may bow down and touch our brow with the kiss of the immortals. It is gradually beginning to be realized that it is not enough to give vent to one's temperament, to pour one's sentimentality over the radiantly objective nature of the worlds around us. These worlds are diminished by our pressing of them into the narrowness of our own subjectivity. In that case we render only a personal reflex instead of their own brightness and life. We express not their own being but what we have made of them within our own world of feeling – a reflected image coloured by our own emotional state of mind. Have we any right to do this? Has the poet captured in words nature and the forces lying behind it, and given them plastic shape and form, so that we can destroy them and put something personal in their place? The personal element is not always *sufficiently worthy of being pushed into the foreground*. From what murky source does this reflection often stare out at us? What a sad metamorphosis is all too often wrought! *Voluptuous soul desires* and brutality scream, hysteria performs its wild dance, triviality suddenly deadens the din, wasting away insipidly in an expiring void . . . But how do we come close to the essence of things? How do we release the powers of the spirit from out of the words?

In the words themselves lie the forces which, if we can feel our way into them, conjure forth a lost paradise. *It is said of the Word that* it created all worlds. The whole power and significance of

* In italics.

the Word must dawn in our soul. Every sound, every tone must be recognized by us in its manifoldness and splendour. It must go through our consciousness filling it with the thrill of reverence. No subjective shade of feeling is needed to express the fact that the sun shines, the moon gleams, the stars twinkle, winds blow and waves billow. In the sounds themselves lie the creative forces that set objective life free if we heed them and resist the urge to express instead our own attitude to sun, moon and stars. Creative power still lies in the Word, but we have lost the key to the Word. Our language has withered; sounds and syllables drop away, word structures expressive of the spiritual disappear. Ahriman stretches out his bony hand and forms through our mouth, through our pen, word structures that entangle us in matter. Do you not see the toothy grin of Death with his sickle? Between these teeth the word turns to pulp, and like a distant plaint there echoes from a remote past the sound that once by science and art was conjured forth from stone massif to greet the rising sun.

A magnificent symbol. In those days stone was treated in such a way that ensouled sound was set free from it. Now, however, man is treated as a mechanism. In the most recent methods of speech training the pupils are made to speak into a mechanical device. The recording is played back to them a month later so that their progress in the meantime can be assessed. This is the most soulless thing modern technology has produced. It has banished soul and spirit. The spectre of the voice, bereft of spirit, is taken as measure for the training of the living human voice. And other methods in use are much the same – physiologically mechanical even into the most refined subtleties, killing the spirit, driving out the soul. If, for instance, the vocal cords are strengthened and stabilized through irradiation, it is at the cost of mellowness and transparency in the voice – a hard, tight, mechanical sound being the result. The modulations of the voice are lost, the fine gradations of light and shade obliterated.* In lieu thereof one has to hold forth

* The following entry was found in one of Marie Steiner's notebooks: In a school for recitation in Hamburg the training takes two years. First year only

with temperament or plaintive sentimentality and if this is discounted one simply does not know what to do. One hears, for instance, in first class theatres nowadays Marys who talk down from their pedestals like washerwomen at the tub –. hard, unmodulated, earthy and unrhythmical. One cannot expect more from a washerwoman because this is the tribute she pays to her work. But ought someone who represents Mary – raised above all earthly gravity and descending from spiritual heights – ought not she to find other qualities in her voice to express heavenly grace and gentleness?

Nasal resonance, which increases the power and range of the instrument, also leads to monotony. There is a complete lack of the delicate intervals, the divisions of a tone, quarter tones, eighth tones, which have so many more intimate degrees in speaking than in singing. And when an instrument schooled in the way mentioned above is used to speak in a soft and subdued manner, one experiences that the metallic element of the voice, cultivated with the help of the nasal resonance, withdraws but then slips back like a beast of prey with velvet paws. It gives the feeling of something unreal, untrue.

In tongue technique also a mannerism is introduced that has the effect of being superficial and untrue. Transitions from a gentle wheedling tone to sudden outbursts of force are remarkably harsh and abrupt and have a brutal effect. This is, once again, the result of technique *separated from the element of soul*. If a voice has the effect nowadays of being especially engaging and full of soul, you can be almost certain that the speaker will say to you that he has no technique, meaning no speech training in the modern sense.

It has been very popular in recent decades to seek speech training from singers. They asserted intrepidly that whoever can sing can also speak. This only provides evidence of how little notion people have nowadays of what artistic speaking really is.

---

technique, no roles or poems may be studied. The voice is placed. Then irradiation – X-ray, everything is measured. Dr. Steiner said to me: through irradiation of this kind the voice is made more sonorous but the organs become cartilaginous.

Singers of the recent past indulged in a mechanical training of the voice and produced countless methods of breathing, which were the ruination of innumerable voices. But apart from this the focal point in training for artistic speaking lies in the giving of shape to the sounds of speech and not, as in singing, in the formation of tone. The voice must be differently 'placed'; or rather, quite a different course must be followed for forming the voice from that usually called the 'placing of the voice'. That is to say it must be allowed to take its course. Let it take its course quite freely in differing ways, through the vowels and combinations of consonants, hither and thither, forwards and backwards, and always into the surrounding air, where it captures what lives and sounds there. The sounding air comes to meet the voice. One only has to hear it. The vocal stream taking its course through the organs of speech must give shape to what lives in the air, waiting for it as it were in order to make its appearance. God breathed the living breath into man, who thereby became *earthly* man. Air is in him, a part of the air that has its being outside him. With as little hindrance as possible he must let this, his air-being, flow out into the air surrounding him. He must hear as it were what sounds around him and, capturing it, make it audible to the physical ear. *The organs must be trained through the shaping of the sounds themselves. 'Normally' trained organs must not be made into tyrants over the word.* Speech is a gift of the gods. Every sound has creative forces. It is the task of the speech artist to trace their spirituality and to obstruct this spirituality as little as possible through *his own personal reactions*. He has to allow the creative formative forces to play their role and he has to reach for and awaken a feeling for the life-creating *formative forces* in the sounds, the parts of the Word that have been lost.

How often have singers approached me to ask advice about the voice placement mechanics which were tying them up in tighter and tighter knots. The life of art was lost to them. 'Sing into the mask' was the battle cry of recent times. They created an expression compatible with what they then superimposed as chest resonance and head resonance. The facial expression that

131

people were accustomed to assume in order to take into their consciousness this head resonance complied exactly with the expression 'Sing into the mask'. Let it be clear what that means: cutting oneself off from the external world, encapsulating oneself in one's own personality, going further and further away from a sympathetic *experiencing of the world* and more and more into oneself. Art, which is there to connect us with the eternally spiritual, becomes a means of enmeshing us more deeply in the narrow personal element, in the mask.

It is true, song and the art of speech have a certain point of contact and then go their several ways. The singer must nowadays learn articulate speaking, because he does not merely sing musical notes but vowels and words. Within the word he seeks *to condense the spoken sound into musical sound, while the speaker has to restrain the melody,* in a manner of speaking, by making differentiations within the musical note. For that reason the singer must take a different path from the speaker. He weaves in the element of musical tone. But pure tone is formed and also dissolved in the throat. Singers deny that tone is formed in the throat, but this is an error that prevents them from achieving what the nightingale achieves. The throat must provide the basis for musical tone while the spoken sound is moulded by the other parts of the organism of speech. One should sing musical notes, not vowels. The spoken sound can actually not be sung but it can be used to produce a musical note. The ideal of the singer lies in obliterating speech and becoming a nightingale, which does not speak but sings. Artistic speaking seeks to obliterate the nightingale and allows the gesture of movement in the sound to predominate. This gesture is determined by the content and rhythm of word and verse. For that reason it is often painful to hear a poem sung, as the concentrated thought content in the poem is swept away and the line of movement required by the inner rhythm is wiped out. Language is formed in accordance with thought and has to be subjugated to it, while musical sound is drawn out of the element of will. In music everything remains at a tonal level, while in speech the musical structure has to be adjusted according to the content. Sound would have to remain pure musical sound if it were to fulfil its spiritual mission, but, by combining with the content of language, by entering into a compromise with it in the word that is sung, it falsifies its own nature. The soul casts into the sound waves which darken its very being, alienating it from its spirit origin and making it the bearer of feeling. The word that is sung gives opportunity for hurling out the passions of the soul with the whole weight of the will, unchecked by the reins of thought. While the strongly sculptural forces of word-formation allow the ugly to appear ugly and the beautiful beautiful, the intoxication produced by musical harmonies draws the soul ever more into the vortex of sensuality. Music such as that in 'Salome' is not inspired by the muse but by the courtesan. It is estranged from itself.

The reciter will perhaps, when he has become aware of the spirit power of speech, be able to show the singer the way towards the overcoming of 'the mask'. But to that end he must go his own way, unimpeded by the methods of the singer, a way now lost to him. This way does not lie in the whipping up of one's own over-heated temperament with the help of sonority, but it lies in the formation of speech, in the articulation of its sounds, in the graphically sculptural and in the imaginatively ensouled, *which is at the same time 'restrained' melody*. In the forming of the sounds the speaker must become conscious of his instruments of speech and follow up the lines of resonance. The organs of speech only provide the basis for the creation of vibrations. The basis of resonance lies in the air, the external air in which one must *feeling* hear the sound and *hearing feel it*. All seeking for resonance in nose, diaphragm, chest and head only leads to mechanization. Imitating and learning to listen to the sound is the only correct method in speech. In the good old schools you were only allowed to imitate and you had to go through this first in order then to find your own way. Only after learning to hear can you learn to speak.

Musical sound is as yet inarticulate will. *Speech sounds are organized by thought*. In between lies eurythmy. It is 'Gemüt,' an element of soul that is not yet frozen, sound that is not yet thought but held in the line of the body.

Eurythmy is the region in which there is interplay between speaking and hearing. Listening consists in suppressing what wants to live in response. What the listener suppresses makes its appearance in eurythmy. It must of course be a positive and not a critical listening. Affirmation of that which one hears is what is performed in eurythmy.

Recitation is the adapting of oneself to rhythmic form. When it inclines more towards song it is recitative, when more towards prosaic language it is rhythmic speaking. In a poem it is important above all things to pay attention to the form; the right treatment of the content then comes of itself. In prose it is necessary to work more towards content and to read rhythmically. Novalis has rhythmic prose which should be spoken with differentiated rhythm. With Hölderlin concessions must also be made to rhythmic prose.*

AN ESSAY – 1926

A dear, good anthroposophical friend, whom I seldom see, said to me once many years ago: 'Why does one actually write poetry? To say in many words what one could say in few!'

Shattering! These words struck deep, not because of their

---

* This article was never finished. At the same time (1921) Marie Steiner was working on the article *Aphoristisches zur Rezitationskunst*, which had been requested by the editors of the periodical *Die Drei*, Stuttgart, for their Congress number. A public congress *Kultur Ausblick der anthroposophischen Bewegung* (Cultural Outlook of the Anthroposophical Movement) took place in Stuttgart in 1921 from 28 August to 7 September. It is easy to assume that the article printed above was written down first, since both pieces of work arose in co-operation with Rudolf Steiner and show important additions by him. Perhaps the content was worked over again by Marie Steiner with a view to publication, to draw attention to the general situation in the German theatre of that time. The article *Aphoristisches zur Rezitationskunst* was published in 1922 by Der Kommende Tag, Stuttgart, as a special issue and was taken over after their liquidation in 1924 by the Philosophisch-Anthroposophischer Verlag, Dornach, at the express wish of Rudolf Steiner. The document is still available.

content of truth but because they burnt right into my soul. I thought: what has become of human beings, even those who have come to Anthroposophy? The poet! Poetic word, concentrate of spirit! The poet incorporates poetically into the word the essence of being. It lies like the creative power of growth within the seed, a power that entices forth from the soul a living development, a fruitful projection beyond itself. What would world history be without poetry? It has gathered together events in picture, sound and colour, and so given them permanence. Events would have been forgotten had the power of poetry not contained them in the Word. They remain like polished gem-stones in artistic settings, refracting rays of light, sparkling in myriad ways, stirring amazed generations to admiration and ever and again spurring them on to action, to the emulation of what is great, what is worthy of imitation.

Thus poetry had the effect of being educative and formative, laying the foundation of civilizations and helping them to develop. Young humanity drew from life-giving sources what formed its soul, gave shape to its spirit. It was drawn upwards with the aid of great ideals, which descended to it from divine pastures and were held fast in the word of the poet. The coarse and uncouth actions of humanity's strongest sons were glorified and elevated through it, losing their momentary value and qualifying now only as memorials to the spirit of the age. A tapestry was woven of their deeds and continued to delight their weary successors. Who asks whether it reflects realities? It is art, hence life, and a break-through to the spirit.

All the arts grew out of it. Pictures surged forth and took on shape and surface form, emanating their fragrance of soul in colours. The language of the gods, captured in verse, sought its way through movement and overflowed into activity of the limbs. The microcosm tried to reflect the ways of macrocosmic occurrence – the dance of the planets, and the standing and hovering power of the fixed stars – by arranging its possibilities of movement strictly in accordance with their laws. Thus dance arose and from its radiance stemmed activity of soul and spirit; singing sounded forth from it and became music.

Music, however, inclined towards form. It wanted to consolidate its striving forces, to confine its urge for expansion. It sought its way through space tentatively, set supporting forces free and became architecture.

Thus all the arts clustered round their mother, poetry, to whom they owed their life and by whom they were nurtured.

Were we to speak of rhetoric, of eloquence, or even indeed of grammar, we would find they were enkindled by the poetic word, by formed language.

How far humanity has come from the powers of its youth! How old it has grown! It no longer feels the pulsating, impulsating forces of poetry, no longer knows the ways towards the fountain of youth.

But, to be sure, what is nowadays called poetry has also lost these ways. It has cut itself off from the supporting spirit. It no longer incorporates the spirit but at most its soulful and subjective yearning for it. This subjective element of soul – separated from the spirit, subjugated to the senses, lashed by shredded nerves – allows its wings to droop till they drag in the mud.

So it need cause no surprise if these tired wings can no longer keep up with the frantic tempo of our times and no one actually reads poetry today, or, let us say the 'mostly man', the man in the street. (The 'mostly man' is an expression used by a railway official who could not understand why Rudolf Steiner and I once took the slow train at night after a lecture. The 'mostly man' travelled with the express that followed shortly after.)

The man in the street has no time for poetry today and looks on it as word-skirmishing. Unfortunately he is all too often right. But even advanced theosophists often have a poor opinion of poets and poetry. I remember a lady, the 'most advanced' theosophist of a certain country, the English representative in Italy of ancient wisdom, destined to be the 'soul' of Theosophy in that country – among the jostling male representatives of the theosophical spirit, there was mostly such a soul as this, who had them all under her thumb and was a kind of missionary-extraordinary just for this purpose – the soul of

136

just such a foreign land said to me with the most disdainful tone of which an English tongue is capable: 'Oh – poets!'. . . . Further words were superfluous. Poetry was finished and done with and I saw no point in making any effort to revive it.

And yet, in that land, a Dante spoke, and united the dance of the heavenly hosts in the heavenly rose, not merely as image, but as the fruit of knowledge. In him the living source welled up in radiance to the light.

He who brought us light also gave us poetry. But it was difficult to pave the way for an understanding of this in the Society. The doors were barred. It was a long and arduous task against obstacles and misunderstandings, which arose simply from a lack of knowledge. And it was not surprising that the erotic trash of the turn of the century was not to the liking of those good people who sought the spirit out of the need of their souls, or out of their destiny. They did not bother to seek the blue flower in this wilderness of weeds.

I remember how gently the searching eyes of Rudolf Steiner shone when he once asked me, in the early days of our work together, which poets I liked best among the moderns and I had to reply that most of them did not interest me but that I would choose to fall back on Jordan and Hamerling, who interested me especially at that moment because of their epic power and objectivity. He seemed surprised and was pleased and told me many things from his recollections of these men.

He gave me free rein and, as I now know, watched with interest when, after a literary tea I gave in Berlin, I once wrote, as I felt my duty demanded, to the poetess who had been reciting, saying that I had been very shocked by her poems and by her manner of delivery and could not refrain from giving expression to the view that what she had chosen as material and manner of presentation could not possibly point to the purpose and meaning of poetry. She replied loftily: 'Whoever speaks of purpose in poetry shows that he is blindfolded, and this prevents him from seeing what is truly beautiful.' Rudolf Steiner's behaviour was kind and restrained on this occasion and we soon agreed to discontinue the teas, which he regarded as an unfortunate inheritance from the Theosophical Society. A serious movement could not be built up through teas and earnestness ought to come into our Movement. Yes, it all depends on what is put into verse and how form and content correspond.

At that time I did not know Conrad Ferdinand Meyer, that master of form. I learnt to appreciate him when the sculptural power of eurythmy compelled me to chisel the word in sound. How his strongly-formed structures curved and zig-zagged, expanded and contracted. How contoured and chased they were, solid and strong like granite, glittering like mica schist, lush as an alpine meadow. A lot has been written about his having taken his form from the French, but he has it from his mountains, from their bold contours and stony core, from the perpetual snows and the brilliant light of the heights, which compel him to cast aside all that is useless. He has within him the pure air of the mountains and the resinous and spicy tang of the fir trees. He has the gentle power of the meadow, the frothing foam of the waterfall and the transparent depth of the lake and much, much more. He has the weaving life of nature in its elemental spirituality. He hears voices murmur and he sees misty structures condensing and acquiring form and lustre and colour. There is substance in his poetry and genuine truth. But they say that he was neurotic. They speak, whilst acknowledging his undeniable significance, somewhat ashamedly of the mental institute and of spiritual night. There was day in him, bright day, and the surrounding night thrust the brightness back into his soul. He could not force his way out until, after forty-five years, the spirit broke through by means of form, by means of the concentrate of poetic word. Once the spark has flashed out from this granite form it is felt from then on purely as spirit.

Who has not seen the Matterhorn from the Gornergrat in the most wonderful early evening light? Depending on the wreath of clouds and play of light that surrounds and floods it, this apocalyptic structure of nature at one moment looks like the recumbent body of a lion, with great gigantic paws curved in front of its avalanche-breast, with human-like profile in the jagged formations of its heights. Then again it has the buoyant swing of the eagle's flight in the icy-blue, furrowed, steeply falling slopes. We find it once more in the mighty grip with which the poet takes hold of history and turns it into poetry. Words are the equipment of the poet. The poet is he who compresses mighty content, condenses, makes poetry, concentrates in such a way that the word acquires the power of a seed that germinates in man's soul, bringing civilizations to flower, and through the centuries and millennia inspiring man and endowing him with life.

APHORISM

Rudolf Steiner has described speech to us as that in which man grasps his divine nature; through it he raises himself above the animal. It gives him shape and form. It pulsates through him with its forces. It gives him his countenance. In it there live the forces which once formed the cosmos, which worked through the cosmos on the microcosm, Man, and made him the very image of God. A primal language once bound all people together. Differentiation came with the Fall. Language became the dividing factor through which people no longer understood each other. The loss of the unifying bond led to enmity amongst nations, now divided into linguistic groups. But the unifying element continued to live in the sounds. As soon as one goes back to their ground and origin they are the same in all languages – seven planetary vowel forces and, corresponding to the twelve signs of the zodiac, twelve consonantal powers. In some older languages we still find strict adherence to this arrangement, for instance in Finnish, which knows no modification of the vowels and does not divide the consonants into hard and soft ones. This differentiation is no doubt produced by a later transformation of speech. The manifesting, creative powers of language live in the planets and in the fixed stars. Their form-creating powers, which give direction, lie in our sounds. Artistic speaking has the task of recognizing these spiritual laws and making them manifest.

FOR THE ACTORS

There is still even now a lack of direct experience. Everything goes through ideation. This then whips up emotions, resulting in much coarser effects. Finer perception arising from within, which could grasp the word directly, is thus lost. The lifeless reflex brought about through ideation has a sharp and jagged edge. What follows must lie in what has gone before.* If it does not do this then there is a lack of artistic necessity. Things suddenly stand there, unexpectedly and abruptly, whilst otherwise they are developed organically with all the delicate nuances that lie in the transitions.

To this end we must plunge down into the very essence of things and allow them to come into being. We must listen to them: they speak. For that reason we must frequently let them run off our lips 'sotto voce', listen, and adapt ourselves to them without letting our ideas interfere.

The things themselves then speak out of the sounds, prompting us to the right word. They work correctively in our own creative activity.

People listen nowadays to words in poems just as little as to other people in conversation.

EXERCISE FOR MY PUPILS

For control of the breath, for speaking in the stream of the breath with a conscious forward-stepping movement. To be spoken only in the air. There are no thoughts, no feelings – only an experiencing of the flower. Nevertheless there is perhaps some sense in practising this poem because it is impossible to speak it sentimentally.

---

* *Das Künftige voraus lebendig* – 'the future living in advance' – these words from Goethe's *Vermächtnis* were a kind of motto firing the actors in their daily work.

Die Klematia spricht:	The Clematis speaks:
Leis schaukeln im Lufthauch,	Soft shaking in breezes,
Zum Vierblatt gerundet,	Four petals are rounded
Violett-tief die Kelche	In deep violet cups
Der schlanken Klematis	Of the slender Clematis.
Von Purpur durchglutet;	The purple glows through them,
Goldschimmernd das Herz.	Heart shimmering with gold.
Sie zittern im Zauber	They tremble in magic
Der Sonnendurchlichtung,	Of sun shining through them
Der Farbendurchwirkung,	As colours work through them;
Entsprossen dem zarten	Shoot out of the slender
Aufstrebenden Stengel	Slim stem striving upwards
Von schwungfroher Kraft.	With strength of glad swing.
Ihr schmächtiger Pfeiler,	Her slim slender pillar
Hinströmend die Selbstheit	Streaming forth selfhood
In dauernder Bildung	In continuous structure
Fünfblättriger Zweigung –	Of five-leaf-like striving –
Klimmt auf zur Vollendung,	Climbs to completion,
Getreu dem Gesetze	True to the law
Hingebender Liebe	Of love in surrender,
Kraftwirkender Güte –	Of strength wrought by bounty,
Empor zu dem Lichte	Up to the light
Gestaltenden Äthers.	Of the shape yielding ether.
Und siehe das Wunder,	Behold ye the wonder,
Es hat sich erfüllt:	It is now fulfilled:
Gewandelt hat sich	Transformed in itself
Der Treusinn des Grünen	Is the faith of the green
Zum Ernst des Violett!	To the earnest of violet!
Die herrlichste Blume	The most glorious flower
In sinniger Schöne,	In appropriate beauty
In hehrer Strenge,	In rigour so splendid
In milder Tiefe	In gentle profoundness
Sie winket hernieder	It makes a sign downwards –
In farbfrohem Klang,	Sound joyous in colour –
Sie leuchtet im Feuer	It shines in the fire
Der göttlichen Andacht	Of godly devotion
Sie schimmert im Lichte	It gleams in the light
Der menschlichen Ehrfurcht,	Of man's veneration,
Sie spricht von der Einung	It speaks in the union
Der Kräfte des Finstern,	Of forces of darkness
Der Kräfte des Lichts –	Of forces of light –
Zu inniger Bindung	To innermost binding
Erdleichtesten Stoffes	Of earth's lightest matter

Mit strahlendem Schein;	With radiant glory;
Zum lösenden Dreiklang	Resolving on triad
Der Stoffesdurchkraftung	Of strength filt'ring through matter
Der Seelendurchichung,	Of 'I' filt'ring through soul
Der Ichesdurchsonnung	Of Sun filt'ring through 'I'
– In Geistselbsterfüllung –	– In Spirit-Self fulfilment –
Erlösend das Wort.	Redeeming the Word.

NOTES ON STAGE DIRECTION

Language as total organism is a fully sentient human being. We could also say: a whole gathering of fully sentient gods.

We must develop an intimate sense of hearing for silent speech, and attain to such an objectivity in speech that we give utterance to what has been inwardly heard. Then we come to the point of living in the words and our whole concept of life is raised to a certain spiritual niveau. That gives us a sense for artistic form. –

When we hear with the soul, we reach the right conception all the sooner – pictorial interpretation instead of interpretation according to ideas.

Inward listening in soul is a kind of intuition. Do not rehearse intellectually by so-called pre-occupation with the content, but hear the respective rôle beforehand.

*

Express the relationship of the character to his inner or outer surroundings. The actor is the ego-centre of his surroundings, with cosmic forces flowing through him. He radiates these forces out again, but now tinged with an individual kind of mind and spirit depending on the character to be portrayed and the words through which the poet expresses his intentions. –

Etheric and spiritual lines of force radiate around man, which meet and unite with the objects and spirit-realities in his surroundings. The act of grasping is the intensive will-impulse to take strong hold of one's thoughts. (This is a Michaelic impulse.)

*

When divine occurrence is given utterance through the human individuality, the linear movement goes into the 'condensing' of the ego. The breath therefore streams downward – in the thematic line. For instance: *Das Tier, die Pflanze, diese Wesen hatten . . .**

When the ego surrenders, and returns to its source, it takes the 'depth' with it, but the tone is continually being fined down, and the ego follows the tone in expiration upwards: *Da nimm. . . ,*† *Wie in lauter Helligkeit . . .*†

FRAGMENTARY NOTES

The experiencing of the word leads to intimacies in spiritual knowledge, which work like the breaking of a seal to the mysteries of Man. Within the realm of language man comes to meet us out of the very foundations of his innermost being, built up out of the forces of the cosmos, which have in their sounds their gesture-language, their sounding signs. The forces of the zodiac and the forces of the planets are compressed into the sounds. They work in them, and owing to their sounding together in man, press forward through man to new states of consciousness. In man they have made themselves a likeness into which they have entered and through which they would manifest themselves again and again in ever-changing interplay but under primordial, eternal, divine sway. This ruling of the divine can be apprehended through the experiencing of speech. Its laws are caught and controlled by the breath (this inner 'air-man') becoming conscious of itself as an instrument for weighing and measuring the directions of space, the march of time and the forming forces of feeling. One can let this instrument, this inwardly activated stream of one's own breath, fathom the depths of the external element of air like a plummet. One can feel, taste and grasp this element in its pliable, delicate, flexible, resilient and formative power. One can sense the chiselling, modelling, sculpturing force of the stream of one's

* Refrain from *Ich und Du* by Christian Morgenstern.
† From *Wir Fanden einen Pfad* by Christian Morgenstern.

143

own breath, activated and consciously guided through the impulse of the will. The breath is given the power to control and give contour to this element of air until one thrusts through to the spirit. There is an experiencing of oneself as breath-being. 'God breathed the breath of life into man' and only then did clay become man. But this cannot be thought out, it must be known through experience. . . . And he became a living soul. . . . But how does he become spirit? Through the awakened ego-force, through the grasping of consciousness in the 'I'. Man must have emerged from that which makes him a separate, enclosed being into that which connects him with the whole universe, which reveals to him the forces of his own origin, of his own structure, of his own goal. For the personal man knows nothing of the goals the ego-man has set for him. He can only slowly and gradually decipher the script with which his own destiny confronts him.

Artistic work helps us in this, for art reveals to us the secret laws of nature, and the secret laws of nature lie deeply anchored in the rule of the divine. We can dip into these divine laws if we work with that within ourselves which is least removed from the inner aspect of the spirit and to which we can still attain with our consciousness. That is first and foremost the breath.

Let us follow our breath: its rhythmic expiration leads us outwards, and takes us with it, spreading us out into the world's expanses. Then we draw back into ourselves, but in drawing back we have taken into ourselves the external objective world, the element of air that bears it, determines and holds it. A piece of objective world has come into us, has shone through us and filled our senses, has united itself with our warmth and has thereby become our own being, a part of our own being, in as far as it gave us life. It speeds outwards again in order to take away from us that which would give us death. It hastens outwards and is dispersed again into the world's expanses. Alternation, rhythmic beat of the wave; we grasp it with our breath and know that we are not in ourselves unless we take the world up in us, that we are more in the world than in ourselves, in our own organism. This knowledge brings light into our breath, inner light, a light which penetrates our external sense perception. We feel our senses as a refined breathing.

JOTTINGS FROM NOTEBOOKS

The ego-organization plays on the wonderful musical instrument of the astral body.

Through the structure of language we learn to know the ego-organization.

By studying the genius of language we learn to know the ego-organization.

In tone eurythmy we call forth those movements that correspond to the formations of the astral body; in speech eurythmy those formations that correspond to the ego-organization.

In carrying out physically the movements for the sounds of music we work consciously on the formation of the soul of man; in carrying out physically the movements for the sounds of speech we work consciously on the formation of spiritual man.

Knowledge must ascend from learning to sculptural activity, to the elements of music and speech.

In ascending from the abstract laws of natural science to that which assumes form as sculpture, one learns to know man in accordance with his ether body.

In uniting oneself with words, not only externally through memory, but through learning to know the genius at work in them, one learns to know the ego-organization.

We must transform cosmic insight into artistic pictures. When concept is rich in feeling it can be communicated artistically.

Expansion of the soul is something that is wrought through knowledge attuned to the cosmos.

The mysteries of the universe must stream pulsatingly through man, as if he were the mere instrument through which they express themselves.

1940

*

One does not approach the etheric world with ordinary artistic thinking and feeling, because the approach to the etheric world is something through which one does not merely look into space, but through which one apprehends space in such a way that the ether makes space empty. In this emptying of space there is an experiencing of the living element. It is necessary to practise quite a different kind of thinking in order to ascend to these higher worlds.

*

Man must place himself consciously into the whole universe in order to grasp himself as a being endowed with speech.

He must learn to sense the directions – the heights, the depths and the circumference. His word carries him far further out than any bodily movement through which he learns to sense space. In his word he lives as air-being, and breaks through the solid boundaries of his body.

How does modern man speak? His brain functions like a physical apparatus, it only reflects. His bony structure transfixes the sound, holds it tightly and binds it. It is actually the skeleton that speaks. Sentiment has to be pressed into it so that an illusory life may be introduced into this bony, mechanical speech. It is drawn out of the over-heated, over-intense personality, at best out of sentimentality. This however always gives the impression of being untrue. On the other hand it may also be drawn out of nervous tension, which leads to ever greater exaggeration, or for the sake of desired effect, to hysteria.

Morbid decadence will soon be out of date. It is being seized upon by mechanization and brushed aside, signifying the triumph of technology over art. It leaps from the screens and from loud-speakers into the limbs and into the voices of human beings.

Here it becomes lignified and lignifies man.

Man no longer finds the way out of himself once he has blocked this living source, which represents his connection with the world around him. The air is both outside and inside him.

The air nurtures his organism. Through transformation it becomes warmth in him and gives him his inner life. Breath makes man a living soul and leads him to consciousness of his connection with the cosmos.

But as long as a voice is only sound, unarticulated or melodious, as with beast or bird, it cannot awaken consciousness. It can do so only when the power of speech is poured into it.

The power of speech is the starry script of the cosmos come to life.

It finds expression in man.

II

RUDOLF STEINER

SPEECH AND THE SPIRIT OF LANGUAGE

GUIDE LINES IN THE ART OF EDUCATION FOR SPEECH FORMATION AND THE TEACHING OF THE GERMAN LANGUAGE

CONTRIBUTIONS FOR A TRAINING SCHOOL IN THE ART OF LECTURING

ON SPEECH DEFECTS

APHORISTIC REMARKS ON SPEECH FORMATION AND DRAMATIC ART

SPEECH AND THE SPIRIT OF LANGUAGE

We speak about the spirit of language, but we cannot say that many people nowadays bring with these words any very clear idea to expression. In using these words one refers to particular and general characteristics in the structure of sound and word, in the construction of sentences, and in the use of imagery. The 'spiritual' factor one then has in mind remains in the realm of abstraction. One simply does not approach anything that deserves to be called 'spirit'.

There can, however, be two ways of discovering the 'spirit of language' in its living power today. The first is revealed to the soul that wins through from purely conceptual thinking to a beholding of what the spirit has to reveal. We have often spoken about this in this weekly publication.* It is an inner experiencing of a spiritual reality. This reality is not to be confused with a mystically indefinite feeling of a general 'something'. It does not contain anything perceptible to the senses, but has as much content as anything the senses can perceive.

He who beholds in this way moves in his beholding away from what can be expressed through language. To begin with his beholding does not find its way to his lips. When he reaches out for words he immediately has the feeling that what he is beholding changes. When he wants to impart information about it, the conflict with language begins. He tries to apply all sorts of possibilities within the domain of language in order to form a picture of what he beholds. He seeks everywhere in the realm of language, from single sounds to turns of phrase. He fights a hard inner battle. He has to admit that language has something like a will of its own. It expresses for itself all manner of things and you yourself must first of all surrender to its will so that it can absorb what you behold. If you want to pour into language what you have spiritually beheld, you do not come up

---

* The essay first appeared in *Das Goetheanum*, international weekly for Anthroposophy and Threefold Order. Vol. I (1921/22), No. 50 (23 July).

against an indeterminate wax-like element that you can form arbitrarily, but you come up against a 'living spirit', the 'spirit of language'.

If one struggles honestly in this way, it can lead to the most excellent results. There comes a moment when one feels that the spirit of language absorbs what one has beheld. The words and phrases on which one alights themselves assume something spiritual; they cease to 'mean' what they usually mean and slip into what has been beheld. Then something occurs of the nature of a living intercourse with the spirit of language. Language assumes a personal character; one comes to terms with it as with another person.

This is one way of feeling the spirit of language as something living. The second appears, as a rule, when treading the first, but it can also be a path taken on its own. You are on this path when you can again experience the original, concrete, fresh, vivid meaning of words and phrases, which have already acquired an abstract character in our time. In speaking the word *Überzeugung* (conviction), the state of mind of having attained to the very truth of a matter is felt. One has already learnt to 'feel one's way out of the word'. In feeling one's way back into the word again *Zeugung* arises – 'producing' in a physical sense. *Überzeugung* becomes a similar process in the realm of the soul. You see what really occurs in the soul when it is filled with conviction.

You should observe words such as *gefällig* (obliging) in this way. What a wealth of inner experience is revealed. Someone who is inclined to 'fall' loses his balance; he shuts off his consciousness. Someone who 'obliges' another, surrenders himself for a moment; he enters into the consciousness of the other one; he has an experience that reminds him slightly of what it means to 'fall' in a faint.

Whoever experiences such things with a healthy mind tuned to reality, without trifling, and without wanting to make witty observations on questionable theories, must ultimately confess that in the making of language there lies intelligence, reason, spirit – a spirit which the consciousness of man does not first put there, but which is operative in the subconscious, and which man simply finds in the language he learns. In this way he can be brought to understand correctly how *his* spirit is a creation of the 'spirit of language'.

All the prerequisites for a search in this direction for the 'spirit of language' lie in the results of contemporary research. Much has already been done; only the conscious building up of a psychological science of language is still wanting. In our circles, however, we must point not so much to a necessity in this direction, but rather to something that has significance for everyday life. He who sees this clearly must surely find that language conceals within itself something that leads beyond it, to the spirit itself. The spirit is not something that can be manifold in the manifold languages, but it lives in them all as something uniform.

This spiritual unity in languages becomes lost when they discard their original, elemental life, and are grasped by the spirit of abstraction. Then the speaker no longer has the 'spirit' within him, but only the linguistic garment of the spirit. The one who says *gefällig*, and feels his way in his soul towards the picture described above, has a different experience from the one who only connects with the word *gefällig* the abstract meaning he has learnt, of the relationship between two people when one 'obliges' the other.

The more abstract the direct experience of language becomes, the more the souls of men will be separated from one another. Each single person has what is abstract as his 'own'. He cultivates it for himself. He lives in it as in his own special ego-hood. This abstract element can only be acquired completely in the realm of concepts. But the experience of word and phrase approximates to it in a very high degree, especially in the languages of civilized peoples.

But we live now in an age when the connecting link must consciously be nurtured over against all the dividing factors which exist between human beings and nations. These separating factors are removed, even between people who speak different languages, when each one experiences the pictorial element in his mother tongue. It should become an important element in social education to arouse the spirit of language in languages again.

Whoever directs his attention to such things will find how many of the efforts called 'social' today depend upon a paying of attention to the life of human souls and not merely upon considerations of external arrangements.

It is one of the most essential tasks of our time that a trend should be set towards mutual understanding in order to counteract the tendency towards this separating of peoples according to language. There has been much talk about humanizing in the sense that the truly human element in man should be nurtured. A striving such as this will only be completely true if it is taken seriously in all concrete spheres of life.

Just think how much more fully, how much more intensively a person feels himself to be human, if he has once carried an absolutely vivid pictorial element into his experience of word and sentence, than one who experiences language abstractly. However, you must not think that someone who says, whilst looking at a picture: it is *entzückend* (delightful) should visualize twitching at that moment, or of being involuntarily carried away until his limbs no longer twitch. (Tr.: the verb 'zucken' means to twitch). However, the person who has once felt this picture conveyed vividly into his soul with the word *entzücken*, will feel differently when he utters the word than the person who has always experienced it only abstractly. The overtone in his soul will of necessity be the abstract, conventional and scientific one of everyday conversation. However, the undertones should not also be so.

During primitive stages of civilization, the people experience their language pictorially. At more advanced stages, however, education must see to it that this pictorial quality is not lost.

GUIDELINES IN THE ART OF EDUCATION FOR SPEECH FORMATION AND THE TEACHING OF THE GERMAN LANGUAGE*

A teacher reported that her class bellows and shouts, particularly in language lessons. The greatest difficulty is probably that you have such a tiny little voice. You must train your voice a little, and learn to speak from 'below'. Don't squeak when you raise your voice. It would be a pity if you did not take your voice in hand so that a darker quality is brought into it. You must get some depth into it.

*

A discussion ensues about certain children whom Rudolf Steiner has seen in the morning.

I would find it very good if you began your lessons with the Lord's Prayer; and then go on to the verses I shall say for you. For the four lowest classes, I would like you to say the verse as follows:

Der Sonne liebes Licht	The Sun with loving light
Es hellet mir den Tag.	Makes bright for me each day.
Der Seele Geistesmacht,	The soul with Spirit-power
Sie gibt den Gliedern Kraft.	Gives strength unto my limbs.
Im Sonnenlichtesglanz	In sunlight, shining clear
Verehre ich, O Gott,	I reverence, O God,
Die Menschenkraft, die Du	The strength of humankind
In meine Seele mir	Which Thou so graciously
So gütig hast gepflanzt,	Hast planted in my soul,
Dass ich kann arbeitsam	That I with all my might
Und lernbegierig sein.	May love to work and learn.
Von Dir stammt Licht und Kraft,	From Thee come light and strength,
Zu Dir ström Lieb und Dank.	To Thee rise love and thanks.

---

* These directions are printed from unchecked manuscripts, in chronological order, as they were given at the Waldorf Teachers' Conferences from 1919 to 1924. See also: Rudolf Steiner, *Practical Advice to Teachers*, 3rd lecture.

The pupils would have to feel it in the way in which I have spoken it. You must gradually make clear to them – first of all they have to take in the words – the contrast between outer and inner.

> The Sun with loving light
> Makes bright for me each day.
> The soul with Spirit-power
> Gives strength unto my limbs.

The first thing you notice is how the light makes bright the day. Next comes the feeling of the element of soul, and how it goes into the limbs. Spirit-psychically – physical-bodily. This is what lives in this sentence.

> In sunlight shining clear
> I reverence, O God,
> The strength of humankind
> Which Thou so graciously
> Hast planted in my soul,
> That I with all my might
> May love to work and learn.

This is added reverently to the two above. Then returning to both once again:

> From Thee come light and strength,
> To Thee rise love and thanks.

I think that the children should have this feeling toward the divine element in the light and in the soul. With this feeling, as I have read it to you, try to speak it with the children in chorus. First of all, the children must learn it purely by rote, so that they have word, beat, and rhythm. Explanation comes later. Do not explain at first, neither lay much stress on the children learning it by heart. They should receive it literally from your lips to start with. If it goes badly for a time, even for four weeks, the better it will go later on. The bigger children can write it down, but the smallest ones must be taught it gradually. Do not insist that they learn it by heart. It is good if you write it down for them, then they have it in your handwriting.

*

Report from Class 6

The children learn to think and feel better, through doing eurythmy, and vice versa.

Let K.B. do eurythmy to certain speech exercises (see p. 46, speech exercises for teachers)

Help E.H. by relating things which stir the emotions.

*

The case of O.R, concerning the theft of copper wire and a scarf-pin: Make children who steal aware of what children experienced in a by-gone age. Let them imagine things from an earlier time; otherwise something in the nature of cleptomania can emerge later. In the case of R. in the 7th class, theft has been proved.

You should make him sit for a quarter of an hour with his feet in his hands as a punishment. Strengthen the memory by letting him think backwards:

> His father reads the book.
> Book the reads father his.

Also reversed numbers: 3426–6243, or Moh's scale of hardness forwards and backwards. Also the speech exercises backwards.

*

There is a report on the special class, and then on language tuition.

Languages are learnt that much more easily, and the pronunciation is that much better and purer, the earlier one begins. The aptitude for languages decreases as the children get older – from the age of seven onwards. Choral speaking is very good, for speech is a social element. It is easier to speak in chorus than alone.

*

I would say it will be a question of general didactic economy how far you go with choral speaking. If too little were to be cultivated, the social feeling developed through it would suffer. If one does too much, the power of comprehension would suffer, because of the suggestive power of choral speaking. When they speak together, children can do things which they otherwise cannot do, just as a crowd in the street is carried away. The younger the children are, the more deceptive it can become. It is good to pick children out at random to do the same thing on their own. The others then have to be attentive while the chosen one is saying his piece. In telling a story, one is dealing with sentences, and one lets one child after another continue. Things such as this have a certain significance – if I say 'the one in the middle row on the left, continue!', or 'the one sitting alone in the corner, continue!'. Such things as this should be done to make the children attentive, and to make them co-operative. Too much choral speaking would induce laziness. This is confirmed in music in connection with shouting.

*

Regarding E.M., a pupil in class 5 who stammers.

Have you already introduced her to me? I would have to see her. One must know the reason for it; whether it is an organic defect, or a psychological one.* It can be either. If it is a psychological disturbance, one could give certain specially-formulated sentences,† in order to train her. If it is an organic defect one would have to do something else. I shall have to see her tomorrow.

*

* See also p. 215 on speech defects.
† See pages 42 and 125.

A question was asked about L.G. in Class 3. She is nervous and stammers.

It would help if you would try exercises with the sounds k and p. I don't know whether we have any. She would have to *step* whilst she was saying them, then she would be able to speak them. It would be good also if she were able to do k and p in eurythmy, but such things need not be taken too seriously, as they usually disappear later.

*

In teaching speech there is a tremendous difference between speaking in chorus and speaking alone. Children speak in chorus very easily, but not so when they speak individually. You must make use of this. We shall deal with this question next year in connection with educational method. You should make children speak separately immediately after they have spoken in chorus. One ought to do this as a basis of learning. This is without doubt the case.

It is difficult to manage the curriculum when children from one class have to have language lessons with children from other classes.

In language teaching it would really be good – though it is not practicable – to have classes with two different age-groups together, so that the one could learn from the other. In speech it is good when the younger ones learn from the older ones. As a substitute you could put good and less good pupils together. It is probably not really practicable, but it is a good thing to bring together weaker and better ones for languages.

*

A question was asked about language lessons in one of the upper classes (Class 9).

At this age, I would try to stress the element of recitation, and from recitation to learn still more about the mastery of speech and language. Use the meaning of expressions learnt by the children whilst reciting for other things.

*

Now, I think that choral speaking is good if done in moderation. Please remember that the group-soul is a reality and that you can never reckon on children being able to do singly what they have been able to do in chorus. One has the feeling that when children speak in chorus it is easier to keep them in hand. Practised in moderation it is a good means of bringing the group-soul nature into activity, but it is not good to hand the children over to the group-soul too much. They cannot do singly what they can do in chorus. That has to be managed more wisely. You must ask the children often to speak individually. It has a great educational value. Do not on any account believe that if the children get restless, you have to make them speak in chorus.

*

Should it not be possible to read something out of a book when teaching English in Class 7? How much time will you have for reading? How could one arrange to read the *Christmas Carol*? It is extraordinarily instructive for every child to have the book, then one can call them out one at a time and let them read to the others, but without any compulsion, so that they work intelligently whilst reading together.

For Classes 6a and 6b something poetic. Prose after poetry.

*

Reports were given on language teaching.

We can try to achieve something by dividing the children into groups, and bringing together those with similar knowledge and capacity.

I believe it would be good in Class 6 to read something printed, a teacher remarked.

How old are your pupils? One would have to look out a moderately long story. One would have to find a story, a short story, something that has some substance, not anything superficial. It would be possible to read something like a historical piece out of Mignet.* The pupils would also learn a lot from it.

We shall have to find a new arrangement for the teaching of languages.

It is also the case here that it is so difficult to satisfy the pupils. In teaching languages one has to ask the pupils questions, but the prevailing view seems to be that the pupils are discontented. They learn most by reading. It is a great help for them to find their way into some continuous text. Learning by heart is only an extra aid. One proceeds, in reading, from sentence to sentence. With small children, always speak.

*

Now, for the timetable in Class 10, we have to consider the following: To begin with, we shall have to consider something like German language and literature. It would probably be a continuation of what you had in Class 9.

I had Jean Paul, a teacher remarked.

You have gone through Jean Paul and have finished with it? The chapter on humour, which was set, is finished, the teacher replied.

It would be a case of your now beginning and continuing with some related study of what one could describe as metrics; poetics. The children will then be able to enter into this on the basis of what they have learnt in connection with Jean Paul. The ordinary pedantic methods usually adhered to must be avoided. It must therefore be treated in a living way in connection with living poetry – metrics and poetics, as one usually calls it, but treated sensibly.†

* F. A. M. Mignet (1796–1884) French historical writer.
† Examples were given from German literature.

In this class you would have to go right through the *Nibelungenlied* and *Gudrun*. Where possible, try to go through it in Middle High German, that is, as far as time allows, but discuss the whole milieu out of which the poem has grown. Discuss its artistic and folk-loristic significance, and – apart from what you read as examples – convey the whole content of these great poems to the children. Also, in connection with the *Nibelungenlied*, of course, give some Middle High German grammar in comparison with the New High German grammar. That at any rate would be the programme. Begin with metrics. That is what you would have to take through in Class 10.

*

Would you recommend a book for me for the study of metrics in teaching German?

They are all equally good and equally bad. Look up Göschen,* one of the worst methods, so that at least you have the succession of ideas. There are no good German metrics and poetics. Bartsch, Lachmann – *Nibelungenlied* – Germanized by Simrock. He has tried to keep close to the original. I have given the elements in a lecture in Dornach,† physiologically based on pulse-beat and breath. One can study the hexameter when one includes the caesura, from the aspect of pulse-beat and breath. It is not possible for us today to develop further the metric theory.

*

Questions about the school library.

Reference to Grillparzer and Hamerling. Hamerling's *Aspasia* as late as possible. *König von Sion* (Hamerling) as soon as you have been through the historical part. You can then let them read *Ahasver* by Hamerling. Lessing when they are fifteen years

* Collection Göschen, G. J. Göschensche Verlagshandlung, Leipzig.
† Dornach, 6 October 1920. Lecture in *Die Kunst der Rezitation und Deklamation*, Rudolf Steiner Nachlassverwaltung, Dornach, 1967.

old. Recently there would have been a reason for taking *Der Zerbrochene Krug*. One does not specially need to take the Prussian dramas. Read Shakespeare in English. In such works as Shakespeare's, we should try to read them in the language in which they were written. However, if people are of an age when normally they can no longer learn the language, they should read translations of works as important as Shakespeare's are for the English language. One should not make children read Racine or Corneille in German – only if there is no possibility of their reading it in French.

Fercher von Steinwand. – 24 books of general history by Johannes Müller. They should get used to this style. They should get used to this kind of diction. Other things could be adapted for children. It is good for children to go through *The Story of Good and Evil* from the Mystery Play *The Soul's Probation*. One cannot, however, give them the whole text.

*

May I ask for a directive on the teaching of Aesthetics?

I would try – the children are between 14 and 16 – to introduce through real examples the idea of the beautiful, of art as such. Metamorphoses of beauty in the style of different periods – beauty in Greece; beauty in the Renaissance. It is of particular importance for this period of childhood to build up with a certain degree of concreteness what is otherwise introduced in abstract form. Such works on aesthetics as those by Vischer and Carriere are but chaff.* On the other hand the child is ennobled if at this age it is given the opportunity of understanding: What is beauty? What is sublimity? What is comedy? How is humour realized in music, and in poetry?† At this age the mind of the child is not yet able to assimilate general ideas. For that reason one should introduce such things as: What does declamation mean? What does recitation mean?

When I gave a lecture on declamation and recitation, I made

---

* Vischer 1807–1887 and Carriere 1817–1895.
† See footnote p. 180.

the discovery that many people did not realize there was any difference. The majority didn't realize it. If you take the way one has to deliver Greek verse – that is the archetype of recitation, because it depends on the measure, on the long and the short respectively. In German, when one comes to the working out of what lies at the basis of the *Nibelungenlied*, it depends on high tone and low tone: that is declamation. You have heard an example – the difference between the German and the Roman *Iphigenia* of Goethe. The German *Iphigenia* must be declaimed and the Roman one recited.

Here also Dr. Steiner refers to lectures given in Dornach – those of 29 September and 6 and 13 October 1920.

*

For the present Class 11 we must consider, to begin with, instruction in literature and history. Now we want to build this up in such a way that in our considerations we connect up what is being newly introduced with what has already been mastered in Class 10. What have we mastered? *Nibelungenlied, Gudrun*, Metrics, Poetics. I should now like to put before you how metrics and poetics should be treated in this class. This is what I have called the aesthetic element in the teaching of art. To begin with in literature, the literary element is to be placed in the foreground, and in such a way that you try to create a transition from the *Nibelungenlied* and *Gudrun* to the great poetic works of the Middle Ages, to *Parsifal, Armer Heinrich*, etc., above all, try to create for the children an enclosed world of ideas, so that through cursory treatment at first, the children learn to know the legend of Parsifal, and to feel that the parts they worked on in the original are isolated examples out of an entire whole.

*

In Class 10 I had the impression with *Nibelungenlied* that I was continually coming up against a stumbling-block, because I do not understand anything of the nature of language, a teacher remarked.

165

Of course, in this case it is difficult to speak in general principles. It all depends on the details. I actually mean that if rightly treated the element of language is always of interest to the pupils.

Something drawn out of the organism of language should always be of interest to the pupils. I am of the opinion that teachers working together can do a great deal of good. For instance: Herr B. introduced some very interesting things in his class, which were of interest to his pupils, although a whole number of professional philologists have ignored them. In spite of the fact that they are rules, these things are interesting. What I had to say I said in my Speech Course.* There I linked up with certain things. It is not possible to say anything in general. Much could be achieved if what each person alone knows could always be imparted to the others. There could be a great deal of co-operation in this direction. It is a pity that there is so much knowledge here and the others do not also learn it. In the college of teachers there could really be a great deal of collaboration.

I don't know any Middle High German, a teacher remarks.

I don't think that matters very much. I knew a professor once who gave lectures on Greek philosophy, and who was never able to read Aristotle without a crib, what is important is the ability to enter into the organism of language. Who after all, is particularly good at Middle High German? The other teachers can tell you a great deal.

My pronunciation wasn't good.

Dr. Steiner then read it.

Not everyone reads alike. It is coloured by dialect. We all speak High German differently. It is important in certain cases not to speak High German as an Austrian speaks it.

Do you mean that one only gives certain examples from the original text?

Wolfram's *Parsifal* is terribly boring for youngsters. Someone among you is making a translation of it. Perhaps you could write

* Rudolf Steiner, *Geisteswissenschaftliche Sprachbetrachtungen*, 6 lectures given in Stuttgart from 26 December 1919–3 January 1920.

to Paris for a book, though you would probably get it more quickly if you asked Herr B. to lend it to you.

You can link up with etymology, remarked a teacher.

In connection with languages, I would rather stress the general aesthetic, moral, and spiritual elements – that is to say the general nature of the content should take precedence over the grammatical element. That is valid for all languages and can be emphasized. It is very interesting to consider a word such as *saelde*, or *zwifel*. Much could be said about them which is related to the human soul.

Could Dr. Steiner please say something from the aspect of spiritual science?

In that case you need only refer to *Knowledge of the Higher Worlds*.* There is much recent material on literary problems – Dornach lectures which were of great interest to Albert Steffen.

*

You see you must admit that there was, basically speaking, no difference between an intellectual understanding and an artistic understanding of the universe until the sixteenth century. Just think – nowadays one pays no attention to it – how even the scholastics took care that the whole layout of their books, apart from the initial letters, was consciously done in an architectonically artistic manner. Until the tenth century there was no strict division between art and knowledge. Nowadays a merely intellectual aspect is given to the children, and they are already poisoned with it in the earliest classes of the school.

*

A teacher had great difficulties with her class.

Much lies in the fact that you cannot speak. In this way you will never succeed. You must make up your mind to take a real speech training. The fact that you were not able to cope stems

---

* *Knowledge of the Higher Worlds* by Rudolf Steiner, Rudolf Steiner Press, London, 1969.

from the fact that you continue to give in in the way you have always given in. You cannot speak. If one is like this in front of a class one will not be able to manage.

That applies to a good many. Mr. X cannot understand this because he has cultivated a way of speaking that penetrates into one's very fibres. You must not underestimate the difference it makes whether or not you take pains to give shape and form to your way of speaking. If one does it instinctively as you do – it is fortunate for you that your speech is effective – you ought not to be surprised to hear that the difficulty lies here. Miss X will have difficulties until she takes the trouble to have proper speech training.

To Mr X: Your speech carries, and on this your whole bearing depends

To Miss X: You will see when you make up your mind to have speech lessons, that your gestures will change. You give the impression of a real old fogey. Mr. X gives the impression of a determined gentleman. Why should one not say these things? Everything depends on it. In education an enormous amount depends on it. – In this respect you must accustom yourself to laying aside everything pedantic if you want to make progress.

If you take proper instruction in speech training you will not have so many colds. I am not surprised. Do not underestimate what a salutary influence being able to speak properly has. Being able to speak properly has great significance. As long as the speech organs are in such a condition that one cannot make use of them – everything is inter-related – as long as the speech organs are not cultivated you will continue to catch cold. I find it dreadful that there are so many colds. If people were really tormented to take a speech training, colds would disappear.

Frau Dr. Steiner: Learning to speak does help one to get over colds, but it is not always so.

But this is in actual fact the case, continued Dr. Steiner. It is an urgent necessity that something is done in this respect.

The question was discussed as to whether Miss X. can and will remain at the Waldorf School. Some teachers made objections.

Miss X: It would be of the greatest importance to me, Herr Doctor, to hear what you have to say on the matter.

I have said what I think. If things go on like this it will lead to immeasurable difficulties. But I would also ask you to realize that what has happened to A. today, could also have happened to B. I believe the situation to be not without its bleaker aspects.

*

A question was asked concerning a deaf-mute child in the special class.

The child is not deaf-mute. The girl hears, and can also be made to speak. The central organ is lethargic. One cannot get through to her, and must try simply everything. Speak slowly to her as an example; make her say everything after you. Proceed in such a way that one does everything slowly to begin with and then speeds up, so that she has to grasp things faster and faster. Also speak loudly to her, getting her to speak softly, then vice versa. Then you do it first slowly, getting her to do it quickly, then follow this with other variations. If possible take a series of words that have a connection, first backwards and then forwards to work upon the centre of thought and speech. Then I would have her do the curative eurythmy exercises applicable to the head daily, even if only for a short time. Apart from this, she should have Edelweiss in the 6th decimal potency, because it works on the connection between the auditory nerve and the centre of hearing. It has a strong effect. It works even where the organs of hearing are sclerotic. You will find that the laws underlying the edelweiss flower (which lies between this peculiar non-mineralization and mineral-materialization) have an extraordinary similarity to the processes underlying the organ of hearing. We have been using this remedy for some years now.

*

A question was asked about a pupil who spoke very softly.
It would be good if, as far as possible, you made him learn by

heart. But use language which is formed, either poetically or in any other way.

*

Our chief trouble is at the moment that if children reach the exam stage with this kind of punctuation things may become unpleasant. In Class 9b they do not punctuate properly. Punctuation depends upon our being able to discuss the formation of a sentence in a stimulating way. This can be done very well during literature lessons.

There is the possibility of showing, for instance, if one starts from the older form of the German language, how gradually the relative clause first appears, purely through the latinization of writing, of literature. This gives, to begin with, a basis for studying the comma. One arrives at a different use of the comma in punctuation if one starts by making it clear to the children that every relative clause must be enclosed within commas. The relative clause leads to interesting discussion, because it is not contained in the older German form. Neither is it contained in dialect. One can go back to the *Nibelungenlied* etc. and discuss how the relative clause is introduced, and at the same time, the first necessity of introducing logic into language. Once one has got hold of the idea of putting relative clauses between commas, you can explain to the children more precisely the concept of a sentence altogether. Then they will have to learn that every clause is separated off by some kind of punctuation. The other things are not so frightfully important. Then one goes on to the elements of thought developed from speech, and arrives at the semi-colon, which signifies a big step. In any case they make full stops.

Now in class 9 it is high time one began. One must be able to work it out from a positive speech formation by entering somewhat into the meaning. This especially must be done in a stimulating way. It must not be boring. Grammar on its own bores them most of all.

In speaking, in dictating, one must make it clear where the

sentences end and begin. One must make this apparent by other means than dictating the punctuation marks. It means a great deal to the children if you accustom them to learning punctuation from the treatment of the sentence. Dictating punctuation is a ticklish business. I would not dictate the punctuation, but let it be heard. It would be much better if one could divide it up in such a way (with the old German language it can be done, but no longer with the new latinized one) that one divides it clause by clause, putting each clause on a separate line.

Without becoming pedantic, one can discuss with the children in a stimulating way the artistic structure of a sentence. Awaken in them a feeling for what a sentence is. Bring to the child's consciousness what a sentence is, so that the construction of sentences becomes something positive. That ought also to be nurtured. One ought to show in graphic form from the style of Herman Grimm that he really writes good sentences. Ordinarily one does not read sentences, but tapeworms – sentences are completely lacking. Arouse a feeling for sentences with shape and form. Herman Grimm writes sentences. There must be a difference between this style of Herman Grimm and that, for instance, which one otherwise reads, say, in ordinary history books. In Class 9 it is essential to arouse a certain feeling for a well-constructed sentence. There is also something else in the curriculum which can be of great use – a kind of poetics. That is left out altogether. No attention is paid to it. I notice that the children do not have a feeling for what a metaphor is. The children must know what a metaphor is, and a metonymy, and a synedoche. Something wonderful can emerge there. That stands in the curriculum and has never been done. This teaching about the trope helps the children to acquire the capacity of giving shape and form to a sentence. This shape and form of a sentence is given by entering into the picture. One can make this clear with the help of examples. For instance, say what this means: O waterlily, thou blossoming swan; O Swan, thou swimming lily. You thereby acquire a clear-cut feeling, through the metaphoric means of expression, of how the sentence is rounded off in an artistic way. It is not at all inartistic, once in a while, to try using writings of good style, to bracket the clauses instead of using commas and semicolons. It is good to bracket one of Herman Grimm's sentences with a red pencil; and then to bracket the less essential clauses with a blue pencil. Then you have a pretty coloured picture of the formed sentence. Then compare such sentences with what one ordinarily writes in the style of newspaper reporting, or German Philistine writing.

*

Some one asked what one ought to do when the children speak badly in class.

Aren't the speech exercises given previously* being used? They ought to have been done earlier in the lower classes. They were most definitely given in order to be done. One notices that the children cannot speak properly. One could also do the exercises which were given for the teachers too, but one must have a feeling for this not-being-able-to-speak properly. We have often spoken about the health-giving aspects of proper speech. One ought to accustom the children very early on to speaking clearly, that has various consequences. During the Greek lessons there will probably be no opportunity for German speech exercises, but in the German lessons the opportunity may well arise. Speech exercises can be done from the most varied aspects at all stages.

In Switzerland actors have to do speech exercises because they have to pronounce various letters quite differently if they are to be understood in Switzerland – the g for example. There is a special 'catechism' in every theatre about the pronunciation of the g.

With regard to Frau Dr. Steiner's proposed course, you must ask for it over and over again. You must wangle a definite time out of her. If you ask energetically enough, something will come of it.†

*

* See p. 46.
† This refers to the exercises given in 1922, which the College of Teachers should also receive.

172

Curriculum for modern languages:

At the beginning of the conference, part of the 9th lecture of the course *Practical Advice to Teachers* was read, and indications already given in connection with the curriculum were collected together.

The language teachers have shown interest in what has already been given. One should not forget that we had certain difficulties in the teaching of languages. Generally speaking, we have had the experience of pupils of various ages coming to us, and of our having to accept new pupils over and over again into our higher classes. We could generally assume that when a nine-year-old child came, it had already learnt something up to a point, but this was not the case with the language teaching. We simply took children into Class 5 who had never learnt a word of French or English, so that basically speaking we were unable to institute a strict curriculum, owing to the way in which we were provided with pupils. It is a question of whether we can go on and arrange it for each separate year, or whether we shall have to be satisfied with giving, in general, certain viewpoints which could be adhered to and carried through all the classes, should we receive into the first school year pupils of a particular kind.

Now our teaching of languages is altogether somewhat free: We regard what takes place in the first two hours each morning as the basis of our education. The teaching of languages must be treated yet more freely in future.

Generally speaking, the child receives instruction in languages, even in Class 1 and up to Class 3 we pursue the teaching of languages in such a way that the child learns the language through speaking it. One should avoid giving the corresponding translation of a word or phrase which the child has to learn. Instead, one should see that the child connects the word or phrase directly with the thing. One should remain in the foreign language and refer to the thing itself and not the mother-tongue. One should continue with this up to the end of the third school year, and during this time it should never even be noticed that grammar exists.

In working with longer pieces one must proceed in such a way

173

that one does not mind the fact that the child makes a verse or a poem its own, purely through the sounds even if it barely understands the text. In an extreme case, the child might learn four, six or even eight lines which it retains purely as sound. Under certain circumstances this could contribute a great deal to the mastery of the language, so that the child eventually learns to understand from memory what it has first of all acquired through sound. In the first three years, poetry is definitely to be preferred to prose. It is clear from the nature of the process, that basically speaking, it cannot be divided up into single years, but that all three years have to be treated in a completely similar way.

Then comes Class 4, when it would be good to begin grammar, not however through the learning of rules, but by making it clear, through the wealth of texts with which the child is already familiar. One should start making grammatical rules inductively, but when they are once made, one should insist on the child learning them as rules. One should not fall into the other extreme of thinking the child should not learn any rules at all, but when they have been deduced inductively, they should be instilled into the child as rules. The keeping of rules belongs to the development of the ego between the 9th and the 12th year of life. The development of the ego can be furthered by the child being given grammatical rules. One can then go over to prose, which should be restricted to a minimum until the end of the third school year. From Class 4 onwards it is possible to transfer to material that can be taken hand in hand with the teaching of grammar – and for that purpose one should take only prose.

We would only make poetry pedantic if we were to extract grammatical rules from it, but prose material can be treated in this way. One can also go over to a kind of translation. It is of course the case that up to now an attempt has already been made to do this a little, but it has nevertheless occurred time and again in class that the dictionary has been used – that one has not sought the connection between the thing and the foreign word, but between the German word and the foreign word. This is of course easier for the teacher, but it leads to languages being treated in such a way in their mutual relationships that the feeling for language is not developed. Now this should begin in the fourth year at school. In Class 4 we should restrict ourselves essentially to the treatment of the theory of word-formation.

In Class 5 we could go over to syntax. In Class 6 we would continue with more complicated syntax, and parallel with this, we would of course always encourage reading. Translations from the mother tongue into a foreign language should not, however, be encouraged. Then short essays, etc. should be written. Translations should be treated in such a way that one says something and asks the child to express the same thing in the foreign language. The child is allowed to say in the foreign language what has been said in German. The teaching of translation could be treated in this way up to the end of Class 6. At all events, one should avoid translating long pieces out of the mother tongue directly into the foreign language.

Reading matter should be discussed, but only reading matter with a lot of humour. One should discuss enthusiastically everything possible connected with the customs, way of life and folk-psychology of the people who speak the foreign language. Information about the country should be introduced in a humorous way, in Classes 5 and 6. Peculiarities of idiom must be noted from Class 5 onwards. Then, from Class 5 onwards, one should include the proverbial and idiomatic treasures of the foreign language, by learning the respective foreign idiom for some situation in life which has been quite differently conceived from that applied in the mother tongue.

In Class 7, things should be arranged in such a way that attention is paid to the fact that a great number of children will leave school after Class 8. In Classes 7 and 8 one should lay stress chiefly on reading, and illustrating the character of the language with sentences. Everything depends on making the things that occur in the life and work of the people who speak the language one's own. This should be practised from texts, and one should see that particular forms of expression are practised through repetition in the foreign language. Only translate occasionally. On the other hand one should make the pupils repeat what one has read – even works with a dramatic content. Dramatic content can be repeated in their own words, but not lyric or epic. However in Class 8 the rudiments of poetics and metrics in the foreign language should be dealt with. A survey of the literary history of the language in question should follow in these two last classes. Then comes Class 9. Then a kind of recapitulation of the grammar would be necessary but treated with real humour, always giving humorous examples. These examples can take you right through the grammar. Stimulating reading should also be given in this class. The metric element in language follows in Class 10, with primarily poetic reading, and in Class 11 a start must be made with dramatic reading. The reading of prose accompanies it, and some aesthetics of language. Poetics should be developed especially from dramatic reading and this is continued for lyric and epic poetry in Class 12. And then we must read especially things relating to the contemporary situation in the foreign country. In addition, we require knowledge of modern foreign literature. This gives the outline of the curriculum to which we should like to adhere in the future.

Do not read extracts without making the children acquainted with the content of the whole work.

In Class 5 or 4 it is possible to begin with the elements of grammar. As far as possible carry on allowing the children to cultivate conversation. With regard to grammar in Class 7 and 8 the following should be said: One should look for a longish passage that one wants to read. First, acquaint the children with the content in a humorous and, if possible, dramatic way, then read the passage itself.

*

The question is asked whether there are the same stages in the teaching of grammar in foreign languages as there are in German.

Well, it is like this. What I have indicated is given according to the needs of the different age-groups. It simply belongs to the different age-groups that one introduces a particular nuance of soul. The child learns to bring these nuances to life most easily in its mother tongue. It would be beneficial to the child if one connected what has been learnt in the mother tongue with the other languages, at the same age. When such moods of soul are given expression, it may be possible to show to what degree deviations exist in other languages. One can by all means enter into comparisons.

You see, one does not begin with instruction in grammar at all until the child is 9 or 10 years old. Teaching of languages is developed at earlier stages purely from speaking, and from the feeling for speaking so that the child learns to speak out of its feeling. At this stage, which is of course, not absolutely clear-cut, between the 9th and the 10th year of life, one begins with grammar. And the treatment of language in connection with grammar is related to the development of the ego. The pursuit of language from the grammatical point of view is related to the development of the ego. It is not a question of asking how to develop the ego from grammar. Grammar simply does it on its own. It is not necessary to give special examples. One simply does not start with grammar any earlier, but tries to develop the teaching of grammar out of the substance of the language.

In Class 8 the rudiments of metrics and poetics should be given, then in Class 11 the aesthetics of language. A teacher asked how that is to be understood.

Metrics treats of the structure of verse. The theory of the structure of the stanza; poetics deals with the theory of the different forms in poetry, the kinds of lyric, the kinds of epic, the kinds of dramatic verse. That is metrics and poetics. Then one goes on to the theory of tropes and figures of speech. Demonstrate this with examples, so that the children have plenty of examples of metaphor, etc.

The aesthetics of language consists in making the children aware – they have by now quite a large vocabulary: German and French, with English as a basis, comparisons may be drawn between the various languages – that aesthetics of language rests upon an awareness of whether the language is rich in the vowels

U and O, or whether it is rich in the vowels I and E. One tries to evoke a feeling for how much more musically rich a language is that has a great many O's and U's, than one which has more E's and I's. One tries to arouse a feeling for how the aesthetic beauty of language declines when the possibility of the inner change of · words through declension ceases. So the structure of language is brought to consideration in aesthetics. Whether it is sculptural or lyric, whether it is rich in complicated interjections, etc., all this differs from metrics and poetics. Aesthetics is concerned with the actual beauty of language.

There is a discussion on the riddle mentioned by Dr. Steiner at Ilkley.*

The first language spoken to the sea is English. The second, the purely musical one, is Italian. The third, the intellectual one, is French. The fourth is the plastic language, German.

Someone asked what lies at the root of French metrics.

Little as one would normally credit it, the sense for systematic division lies at the base of French metrics; the sense for the mathematics of language. That is unconscious. In French metrics everything is intellectually counted, just as in French thinking everything is intellectually counted, only it is veiled by being modified through rhetoric. Understanding here becomes rhetoric, not intellect. It is audible reasoning.

＊

A reading programme is discussed. We have spoken a lot about Class 12. I have given you examples. A certain amount will depend on what the teacher has read, and on what he likes. For that reason I have suggested the qualities needed. Above all lyrics, old and new, should be considered for Class 10.

One teacher says that he started with lyrics of Milton's time and Burns.

You must do it in this way: in Class 10 go through the lyrics of Shakespeare's time and repeat them in Class 12, briefly

* See lecture given by Rudolf Steiner at Ilkley, on 12 August 1923, *A Modern Art of Education*, Rudolf Steiner Press, London, 1972.

indicating their characteristics. You must not leave the lyric poetry of Shakespeare's time out of account because it points remarkably deeply to a period in European development in which the Germanic languages were actually much more similar to each other than they were a few centuries later. English lyric at that time was incredibly teutonic. Shakespeare, when you read him, is not altogether so unteutonic. This can be added in Class 12, so that this feeling arises which for the whole of humanity in general is very important.*

Percy, Shelley, Keats: You must of course choose what you like yourself, because then you will be able to deal with it in a better way. Definite points of view can be given. In English lyric, when it is good lyric, one has almost without exception an element of sentiment. It has an element of sentiment when it is good – sometimes a very beautiful element of sentiment, but an element of sentiment nevertheless. And then the English manner of thought, when it becomes poetic, is simply not suitable for humour. Then it becomes trivial. There is no humour in the higher sense. There is not even a word for it. How should one say *Humor* in English? We would not describe as *Humor* the treatment of Falstaff. There is, it is true, a great deal of humour in it, but we would not describe the whole manner of depicting him as *Humor*. We would notice the unfailing accuracy of the characterization, but that was not felt in Shakespeare's own time. This compactness, this unfailing accuracy of characterization meant nothing to the people of an earlier time. The people of an earlier time were concerned with the fact that they were good stage figures, that they projected well on the stage. Previously people thought more in theatrical terms. One can no longer call Falstaff 'humorous' today. With the word 'humour' one describes someone who dissolves in mist, or rather a person who dissolves into the indefinite – hence dissolves into the mist of his temperament. 'Humour' is the kind

* In this connection we would point out the numerous lectures and series of lectures given by Rudolf Steiner between 1899 and 1905 in the educational institute for workers in Berlin; e.g. *Kultur und Kunstgeschichte im 19. Jahrhundert*.

of temperament one has. The four temperaments are the humours.

Nowadays you simply cannot say that someone has a melancholic 'humour'. So a character which one cannot properly grasp, which dissolves in the mist of its temperament – that is a 'humour'. But what we describe today as *Humor* does not exist in English lyrics. There is no language so strongly imbued with sentiment when it waxes lyrical.*

One should show that as far as the Dramatic is concerned, a zenith is reached with Shakespeare which is never afterwards again achieved. It is of course interesting – but not until Class 12 – to draw attention to historical development, and to the fact that in central Europe the Reformation, the actual Reformation, retained basically a religious character. One can then point out the great significance of church lyrics in German. In France the Reformation did not actually assume a religious character, but rather a social one, and this can be shown from their poetry. In England it assumed a moral-political character, which comes strongly to the fore in Shakespeare. For a long time the English had no idealistic philosophy. This comes out in their poetry, and in order to achieve it, their lyrics needed this sentimental trait. This is connected with the fact that for a long time the English had no philosophy, and this came to expression in their poetry, but that gives their poetry an essentially sentimental trait.

Sanskrit is predominantly rich in the sound A (ah). U (oo) and O (oh) sounds give a language a musical quality. E (eh) and I (ee) detract from the richness of sound quality. The German language is lacking in tonal quality. Sanskrit has something monotonous owing to the preponderance of the A (ah) sound, but it has something which lies between music and sculpture. It has the marked property of becoming sculptural whilst at the same time being musical. That stems from the A (ah) sound which holds a middle position. When Sanskrit has other vowels

---

* See also: *Über das Komische und seinen Zusammenhang mit Kunst und Leben* in Veröffentlichungen aus dem literarischen Frühwerk, Vol. II, Dornach, 1944.

besides the A (ah), they are particularly characteristic. It has a special feature when the Indian intones his threefold Peace, peace, peace. First of all comes the A (ah), then the slight indication, the almost shy indication of the Ego – this is what lies in his Shanti, shanti, shanti. I (ee) is the most strongly egoistic vowel. It is as if one were to blush in face of the ego.

The Finnish language also has many A (ah) sounds, a teacher remarks.

Yes. It depends how long a language remains at a given stage with these particular features. There is, however, something hard in the A (ah) in the Finnish language. This is of course connected with its strong consonants. That is also a hardening, but a hardening which begins to become acceptable. That rests at the same time on a subtle aesthetic feeling for the language. This delicate aesthetic feeling is, however, no longer natural for people these days. If the Englishman were to pronounce the last syllable of his words like a German or a Frenchman, this would result in a hardening. He starts to neglect his last syllables because he passes out of the element of speech altogether. What is a hardening for one person can be something completely natural for another.

A question is asked regarding tropes and figures of speech.

Tropes and figures of speech have an element of imagination. To begin with, you have something absolutely unpoetic. This distinguishes about ninety-nine per cent of all poetry. Then there remains the one per cent. Of this one per cent, poets are obliged, when they wish to lead out beyond the physical plane, to send images and figures of speech soaring above the mere adequacy of ordinary prose. How should one express: O water lily, thou blossoming swan. O Swan, thou swimming lily? What is expressed hovers between the two. What is expressed cannot be expressed in prose. It is the same with figures of speech. But there is also the possibility of expressing the supersensible satisfactorily without imagery or figures of speech, as Goethe sometimes succeeded in doing. Then he does not use an image. You stand right inside the thing itself. That is the case with Goethe, and sometimes also with Martin Greif where what one might call objective lyric is realized. Shakespeare also often succeeded with the lyrics in his dramas.

*

In connection with the speech exercises we would also like to add the exercises given by Rudolf Steiner for children between the ages of seven and fourteen in Caroline von Heydebrand's class:

Was du tust, tue durch deinen tatkräftigen Willen.
Whatever you do, do through your active will.

Gönne jedem Können sein ganzes Können.
Allow each faculty its whole capacity.

Günstig schaue auf künstlerisches Schaffen.
Look favourably on artistic creativity.

Bedeutung suche in jedem Ding.
Look for meaning in all things.

Dringe nicht in das Wasser, wenn du trinkest.
Do not penetrate into the water you are drinking.

Gute Menschen weisen den Waisen wägend den Weg.
Good people show the orphan the way, having carefully weighed the pros and cons.

Was du erfährst auf Lebenswegen weitet dir Sinne und Denken.
Let your experiences on life's way widen your senses and thinking.

Freue dich der freien Natur
Enjoy the beauties of Nature.

Schäume scheinen mehr, als sie sind.
Foam bubbles seem to be more than they actually are.

Schätze ebene Wege, und wäge deine Schritte, dass du wacker wagen kannst, was du vorsätzlich als Ziel dir setzest.

Value smooth paths, and consider your steps, so that you can gallantly dare to achieve the goal you have with forethought set before you.

Die Säule sei dir Wäge-zeichen des Weges.

The pillars are your sign-posts on the way.

Seile winden sich um Säulen.

Ropes wind themselves round pillars.

CONTRIBUTIONS FOR A TRAINING
IN THE ART OF LECTURING

INTRODUCTORY WORDS BY MARIE STEINER

It is peculiar to the German that he regards such things as good style in speaking as trivial and superficial. In this he is wrong. The saying 'Fine feathers make fine birds' has more validity here than in any other sphere. We shall never, it is true, adopt the view held by French speakers that it does not matter what we say, so long as we have discovered how we ought to say it. We should, though, lay far greater stress on this How than we are accustomed to doing.

The words trip out for the lecturer who knows how to speak. He carries his audience away. That is a matter of experience. Why should we not act according to this principle? We serve the content better when we come to its aid through rhetoric, than if we merely say our little piece with the exclusion of all rhetoric.

It is just because we want to give our content its due that we should give it an acceptable form. However our speaking will only be acceptable if we have gone through a training in the art of lecturing.

RUDOLF STEINER

RUDOLF STEINER AS SPEAKER

Rudolf Steiner had the most intense effect as a speaker. He seemed to be endowed with the art of speaking as a natural gift, yet he stressed that he had had to struggle for every sentence and turn of phrase. Although he gave over five thousand lectures, he once confessed that every lecture was for him a sacrifice he had to make. In order to build up a science of the spirit in the language of the present day consciousness, to lay its foundations in such a way that it could withstand the onslaughts of passionate opponents, new modes of thought were required of its founder, new forms of expression had to be sought and subjected to the severest of inner tests. Nothing was to be spoken that had not been thoroughly tested in every respect with regard to its validity. Relevance was the first rule. The listener was never to be overpowered in his life of feeling, never to be influenced through the medium of the will, or by means of brilliant rhetoric. Sound sobriety was the foundation on which a clear, firm thought structure was erected, crowned as it were, with the results of mathematically fine deliberations comparable, for instance, to the cupola of heaven's dome. The element of feeling arose out of the comprehensive extent of his perspective. Dr. Steiner would never give a public lecture on spiritual science without re-sketching in a concise form for any newcomers the basis for an understanding of the lecture. This condensation of immense material to ever more concentrated thoughts, imbued with life, produced an art of lecturing which drew its strength from the spirit, and was wrought – almost beyond the element of time – in short, but all the more intensive moments of concentration. This was certainly preceded, as pre-requisite and preparation, by a youth dedicated to thinking activity, to study and teaching, and to an ever more precise penetration into the nature of the art of lecturing, and the forms it had assumed in the various epochs of history. As he also held courses on the art of speaking, this had become essential.

Beautiful speaking, eloquence, came to Greece from the Orient, from its cultic speaking, and then became rhetoric in

Rome. In the Latin element the conceptual gained the upper hand over the imaginative, and gradually correct speaking became the chief requirement. Eloquence and rhetoric were still retained even in the French language, in fact were brilliantly represented in it, until, through the progressive materializing of civilization, Western pragmatism, the utilitarian point of view cultivated there, became the 'as if' philosophy in central Europe, and from then on, in the element of language, utilitarian import gave the word its colouring. But if the word is to become fully alive and productive again one must go beyond rhetoric and logic to the ethics of speaking. Then one will be able to bring forth new creations again, not merely a renaissance. For spiritual things speech must be freed from opinion and abstract ideas. This can be achieved by observing the context of the statement, instead of merely defining. It is necessary to approach the concrete, living contexts of reality. This leads in turn to good speaking, and in giving the form the appearance of infinity, beauty arises.

FROM THE ORIENTATION COURSE ON ANTHROPOSOPHY, THE THREEFOLD SOCIAL ORDER AND THE ART OF LECTURING

Every detail in an organism has of necessity to be formed just as it is. And so, in the world in which we live, and which we help to shape, everything must be formed just as it has to be formed in its place, in keeping with the whole. You cannot imagine, if you really think, that the lobe of your ear could be formed in any other way than it actually is, in conformity with your whole organism. If the lobe of your ear were formed even a tiny bit differently, you would have to have a quite differently shaped nose, and you would have to have different finger tips and so on.

And so a discourse into which something flows which assumes really new forms must be held in keeping with the whole, just as the lobe of the ear is formed in keeping with the whole.

A discourse cannot be held in the way in which a sermon is held, for the form of the sermon, as we still have it today, actually goes back to the ancient Orient, to the whole attitude man had to language in the ancient Orient. This peculiarity then continued, so that it lived in a certain free manner in Greece, lived abstractly in Rome, and emerges again for the last time in the special relationship the French have to their language. Not that I mean to say that every Frenchman preaches when he speaks, but that a relationship to language similar to that which may well have developed out of the Orient still goes on living, albeit in decline, in the way in which the French handle their language. This element, which we are considering here, came to expression in the study of oratory, for instance, as one could learn it later, though at a decadent stage, from mummified professors who bore the title 'Professor of Eloquence'. Formerly there was such a 'Professor of Eloquence', of 'Rhetoric', in every university, every school, and also in the seminaries, etc. The famous Curtius* in Berlin still officially bore the title of 'Professor of Eloquence', but he got tired of it. He did not lecture on 'Eloquence' but only appeared as 'Professor of Eloquence' because his fellow professors always sent him off to take part in festive occasions. Then Curtius made a particular point of absolving his task on these festive occasions by paying as little attention as possible to the old rules of 'Eloquence'. In any case he was tired of being a 'Professor of Eloquence' in a time to which Professors of Eloquence were no longer suited. He lectured on the history of art, the history of Greek art, but he was registered on the University's list as 'Professor of Eloquence'.

This refers back to an element that was certainly there in ancient times with regard to speaking. However, what is meant by eloquence has not the slightest meaning when we turn to training for speaking in the middle European languages, in the German language for instance. For something has already flowed into these languages which is completely different from what was appropriate to speaking in the times when eloquence was taken seriously. For the Greek and the Latin tongue there exists such a thing as eloquence, but for the German language

* Ernst Curtius (1814–1896), archaeologist and historian.

eloquence is something absolutely impossible with regard to its essential inner nature.

But now today we are living in a state of transition. What, say, was the element of oratory in the German language is no longer of any use. The attempt must be made to get out of this old way of speaking into a new one. And this, in a certain sense, is part of the problem which those who have to speak fruitfully about Anthroposophy or the Threefold Social Order have to solve. For only when more and more people are able to speak in this way, will Anthroposophy and the Threefold Social Order, even in single lectures, be properly understood by the general public, whilst there are not a few who will develop only a pseudo-understanding and a pseudo-acknowledgement.

When we look back on that particular element relating to speaking retained from the times when eloquence was in use, we must say: At that time it was so that speech grew out of man in a quite naive way – in the same kind of way that his second teeth grow. Speaking was a result of the process of imitation, and only after speaking did one come to the use of thought.

Now it was so that man, when he spoke to others, for one reason or another, had to make sure that the inner experience, the experience of thought, slipped, in a way, into what he said. The sentence had structure. In a certain way it was elastic and flexible. The element of thought was more inward than speech. One experienced the element of thought as more inward than speech and then allowed it to slip into one's speaking, so that they corresponded, just as the idea of a statue or the like corresponded to the marble. It was a completely artistic way of treating speech. Even the way of speaking prose was similar in expression to the way of speaking poetry. Rhetoric and eloquence had rules that were not at all dissimilar from the rules of poetic expression. (I would like to add here, to avoid misunderstanding, that the development of language does not exclude poetry. What I now say refers to earlier forms of expression and I would ask you not to take it as if I were asserting that there is no longer any poetry today. It is only necessary to treat speech differently in poetry. But that is

189

irrelevant here; I only wanted to insert this here in parenthesis so that I would not be misunderstood.)

If we now ask how one spoke in this age in which the thought, the feeling content slipped into one's speech, the answer is that one had to *speak beautifully*! That was the prime concern – to speak beautifully. For this reason we can only really learn to speak beautifully by immersing ourselves in the old way of speaking. Beautiful speaking is through and through a gift coming to mankind from the Orient, and it could be said that beautiful speaking lasted as long as the ideal was held that speaking was a singing of speech. Preaching is one form of beautiful speaking, a form however, which has shed some aspects of beautiful speaking. Completely beautiful speaking is cultic speaking and if cultic speaking flows over into preaching something has been divested. Preaching is nevertheless a daughter of beautiful speaking in the cult. Another form, which has come to expression in German and similar languages, is the non-differentiation between word and concept, word and the experience of thought. The word has become abstract so that it behaves as a kind of thought itself. Nothing more can slip in because that which slips in and that which is slipped into are felt from the start to be one and the same.

Who is aware nowadays, in the German language, for instance when he writes *Begriff* (concept), that that is the substantive form of *begreifen* (to grasp), the *Be – Greifen*, hence the act of grasping something, so that *Begriff* is nothing other than the substantive objective view. The concept *Be – griff* was created in an age when there was still a living feeling for the ether body, which takes hold of things. So that at that time one could really form the concept of concept because the taking hold with the physical body is really only a picture of the taking hold with the ether body.

In order to hear in the word *Begriff* the act of grasping, it is necessary to feel language as an organism in its own right. In the element of language of which I am now speaking speech and concept always swim into each other. There is simply not that sharp division there once was in the Orient where language is an organism of a more external nature and where what is spoken lives inwardly. In speaking, what lived inwardly had to slip into the form of the words and, indeed, in such a way that what lived inwardly was the content, and that into which it slipped was the external form. And this had to be done in keeping with a sense of beauty, so that in speaking one was a real speech artist. This is no longer the case, when there is no longer any feeling for the difference between *gehen* (to walk) and *laufen* (to run) in connection with speech as such. *Gehen* has two E's. One wanders along without exertion. E (eh) always expresses the feeling of a slight participation in one's own activity. When one has an Au (ow) in the word, this participation is increased. *Laufen* (running) leads to panting (*schnaufen*) – the same vowel. The inner element stirs, so there must be a sound indicating the change. However, nowadays this is all no longer the case. Language has become abstract like thoughts themselves, which ebb away. This applies to the whole middle region of civilization, but particularly to the West.

In every single word it is possible to see a picture, an imagination, and to live in this picture as in something relatively objective. He who confronted speech in ancient times (the times of beautiful speaking) would no more have regarded language as something not objectively connected with him, into which the subjective element had been poured, than he would have lost sight of the fact that his coat was something objective, and that it had not grown over his body like a second skin. During the second stage in the development of speaking, however, the whole organism of speech was considered as another skin of the soul, whereas speech had previously been much looser – like a garment, I would say. I am speaking now of the stage in the development of speaking in which the prime consideration was not beautiful speaking but correct speaking; in which it is not a question of rhetoric and eloquence, but of logic, in which even grammar itself became logical, to such an extent that one simply developed the logical forms out of the grammatical ones, abstracted them, as it were, from the grammatical. That emerged slowly from Aristotle's time onwards. Everything here merged – thought and word. It is by means of the sentence that one develops the power of judgement. This judgement, however, is incorporated into the sentence in such a way that one no longer experiences it as something inwardly independent. Correct speaking has become the watchword. Nowadays, we see a new element beginning to emerge – applied however in the wrong place, and transferred into the wrong sphere.

Mankind owes beautiful speaking to the Orient.

Correct speaking lies in the more central region of civilization.

And we must look to the West if we would seek the third element.

But in the West it begins to emerge in a quite corrupt form. How does it emerge? To begin with language has become abstract. Word-organism has now almost completely become thought-organism. This has intensified in the West to such an extent that when it is spoken of it is regarded as a joke. But the progress is quite definitely there, although in the wrong place.

In America during the last third of the nineteenth century a philosophical trend opened up called 'pragmatism'. In England it was then called 'humanism'. Its representative in America was James, and in England F. C. Schiller. There are now other personalities busy expanding these things. All merit is due to Professor MacKenzie, who was here recently, for expanding this concept of humanism in an excellent way. Where is all this leading to? (I now mean American pragmatism and English humanism.) They emerge out of a complete scepticism *vis-à-vis* the conclusion that truth is something that does not actually exist. If we assert two things, we assert them in order to give life direction. One cannot produce any special reason for speaking of atoms, but the atomic theory is useful in chemistry as a basis. So we set up the concept of the atom! It is useful: it is helpful! There is no other truth than that which lives in useful, serviceable ideas. – 'God' – It does not matter whether there is one or not, but it is not easy to live without setting up the concept 'God'. It is really easy to live, if one lives as if there were a God. So let us put him there, because it is a useful and helpful concept for living. Where truth is concerned, nobody knows (I am merely recording) whether the earth began according to the Kant-Laplace theory, and will end according to the mechanical heat theory, but it is useful for our thinking to picture the beginning and end of the earth in this way.

That is the pragmatic teaching of James and also essentially the humanistic teaching of F. C. Schiller. After all, we cannot tell as far as truth is concerned whether the human being really has a soul or not. This argument about whether there is a soul or not can go on till the end of the world, but it is useful to assume the existence of a soul in order to grasp all that man does in life.

Of course in our civilization, everything appears, in one place, then spreads to others. And for such things as have arisen in the West as if by instinct, the German had to find something more conceptual, something conceptually transparent. From this arose the 'Philosophy of the As-if'.

It does not matter whether there is an 'atom' or not. We regard phenomena 'as if' there were an atom. We cannot decide whether 'the good' can be realized or not; we regard life 'as if' the good could be realized. The argument as to whether there is a God or not could go on till the end of the world, but we regard life in such a way that we behave 'as if' there were a God. There you have the 'As-if Philosophy'!

These things attract little attention, because one thinks: Well, James sits over there in America with his pupils, Schiller in England with his, and there is Vaihinger, who has written the 'Philosophy of the As-if' – they are a lot of clowns, living in a kind of cloud-cuckoo-land, and what has that to do with anyone else!

But those with an ear for it, hear echoes of the 'as-if philosophy' everywhere; nearly everything people say is tinged with it. Philosophers are funny people. They always spout out those things which other people do unconsciously. An unbiased ear these days seldom hears a person speaking out of his whole heart and soul, with his whole being, expressing himself differently from 'as-if'. But the ear does not normally hear how

193

this 'as-if' lives in the quality and colouring of a person's speech, and how, basically speaking, people are possessed by this 'as-if' in our civilization.

Just as things otherwise become corrupt at the end, something appears here which is corrupt at the beginning, something which must be developed in a higher sense for use in the service of Anthroposophy, the Threefold Social Order and so on.

These things are so serious and important that we ought really to speak about them. 'We use ideas because they are useful in life'. – Everything depends upon raising this triviality of a materialistic, utilitarian theory into the ethical, and perhaps through the ethical into the religious realm. If we want to work in the sense of Anthroposophy and the Threefold Social Order, we stand before the task of having to learn good speaking, in addition to what we can learn from history, i.e. beautiful speaking and correct speaking, and that we develop an ear for good speaking.

I have seldom noticed when I have spoken about good speaking during the course of my lectures – and I have done it very often – that it has attracted much attention. I have always said it does not depend these days upon what one says being correct in the logical and abstract sense, but it depends on something being said or not being said in a particular context. We have to develop a feeling for the fact that something is not only correct, but that it is justified in its context – that it can be good in a certain context or bad in a certain context.

We must learn beyond rhetoric, beyond logic, a real ethic of speaking. We must know how things are permissible in one context which would not be permissible in another.

I may perhaps now give an example that some of you may have noted during my recent lectures. I said then in a certain context, that Goethe had never really been born. I spoke of Goethe's attempts to express himself in painting and drawing, and said that nothing had come of it but that it had then flowed over into his poetry and that again, in works such as *Iphigenia*, and especially in *The Natural Daughter* there is absolutely nothing of an effusive nature. People called these works of Goethe 'smooth and cold as marble' because they are almost plastic and sculptural. Goethe had potentialities which never came to fruition in a human sense; he was never really born. – You see, in the context in which I said that recently it could most certainly be said. But just imagine if someone wrote this in a thesis, in an absolute sense – it would not only be illogical, it would, of course, be totally crazy.

Speaking out of a living context is something different from finding the adequacy or correctness of a word-context expressing the thought and feeling context. To allow a saying, or something similar, to arise out of a living context at a particular point is what leads from the beauty, to the correctness, to the ethos of speech. One feels thereby whether in a certain context one may utter a particular sentence or not.

There is, in its turn, a growing together – but now inwardly – not with language but with what is said.

I would like to call this good speaking or bad speaking. The third form – besides beautiful speaking and ugly speaking, besides correct speaking and incorrect speaking, is good speaking and bad speaking in the sense I have just described. There is a widely-held view these days that you can form sentences and then use them at every available opportunity, because they have absolute validity. There are however in reality no longer any such sentences in our times. Every sentence that is possible in one certain context is simply impossible in another. This means we have entered into an epoch of human evolution when we must of necessity direct our attention to the many-sidedness of human experience.

The Orientals, who lived with their thinking in a quite small territory, even the Greeks, who with their life of Spirit, with their life of rights, and their life of economy lived in a small territory – they also poured something into their speech which looks like a linguistic work of art should look.

What then is a work of art? It is something in which a single finite object virtually appears as infinite. (This is the way beauty is defined even though only partially, by Haekel, Darwin, and others.) The first thing I had to oppose in my Vienna lecture on *Goethe as the Founder of a New Science of Aesthetics** (in the Vienna Goethe-Verein on 9 November 1888) was the definition that beauty is 'the appearance of idea in external form', by showing that one ought actually to say the opposite: *beauty arises when form is given the appearance of infinity.*

And it is the same with language which in a manner of speaking appears as 'restricted territory' – as 'territory' which 'encloses within limits' the possible meaning. When what is actually infinite in our inner life of soul and spirit has to fit into this language, then it must be brought to expression in a beautiful form.

In correct speaking it must be adequate. The sentence must suit the judgement, the concept, the word. The Romans had to do this. Then language was re-shaped from beauty into logic, more particularly as their territory grew ever larger and larger. For that reason the custom has been retained of teaching logic from the Latin language. (And people learnt it quite well that way, too.)

But now we have passed beyond this stage. Now it is necessary to learn to feel language *with* ethos, to acquire, in a way, a kind of morality of speaking in our discourse, by knowing that within a certain context we can either allow ourselves something or deny ourselves something. Here the thing does not slip in in the way I described earlier. Inasmuch as we use the word we apply it to characterize. Then all definition ceases. Then we use the word in order to characterize. Then the word is used in such a way that each word is felt as something insufficient, each sentence as something insufficient. One has the urge to characterize from the most varied standpoints what one wants to present – one wants in a way to go round the matter and characterize it from the most varied aspects.

I have often stressed that that must be the way of presenting Anthroposophy, and I have often stressed that one ought on no account to believe that one could find the adequate word, the adequate sentence, but one must have the attitude of the

* Published by Anthroposophical Publishing Co., 1922.

photographer, who takes at least four views in order to show the tree.

So a viewpoint which gives full rein to an abstract trivial philosophy in the form of 'pragmatism' and 'humanism' must be raised into the sphere of ethics. And then it must come fully to life in the ethos of language. We must learn good speaking, that means we must experience something in speaking of all that we otherwise experience in relation to ethics, the moral doctrine.

Basically speaking the matter has recently become very clear. We have in the speech of theosophists something antiquated, determined simply through the language, antiquated with reference to past centuries of materialistic colouring: 'Physical body' – well, it is dense; 'ether body' – it is thinner, more nebulous; 'astral body' – thinner again, simply thinner; 'ego' – still thinner.

Now there are ever more and more new members of man's being becoming ever more tenuous. In the end we simply do not know how we can still come to these degrees of tenuousness. You never get away from materialism. This is a feature which appears in theosophical literature whenever these things are mentioned. It goes right down from theoretical speaking to what I once experienced within the Theosophical Society in Paris, I think in 1906. A lady, a theosophist right to the very core, wanting to say how pleased she had been with certain talks given in the hall where we were, said: 'There are such good vibrations there!' And one noticed from her that it was actually meant as something that one sniffed. So the aromas that were left from the talks, which one could sniff, were what she actually had in mind.

We must learn to wrest language away from mere adequacy. For it can only be adequate in respect of the material realm. If we want to apply language to the spiritual in accordance with the present epoch of mankind's development, we must set it free. Then freedom must enter into the use of language. If these things are not taken abstractly, but in a lively fashion, the first thing into which a 'Philosophy of Freedom' must enter is speaking, the use of language. This is essential. Otherwise, for

197

instance, the path will not be found which will enable us to characterize the free life in the spirit.

There is as yet very little understanding among our contemporaries for the free life of the spirit – that means life of the spirit arising from out of its own laws. The free life of the spirit is generally understood to be a situation in which everyone cries his own cock-a-doodle-do – where every cock – excuse the rather strange picture – crows on his own dung-hill, giving rise to the most incredible discords. In reality, free life of the spirit gives rise to perfect harmony, because the spirit lives not in each single egoist, but because the spirit can lead its own life over and beyond all single egoists.

There is for example – one simply has to say these things today – a Waldorf School spirit for our Waldorf School in Stuttgart, independent of the teaching staff, in which the teachers must live, and in which it becomes ever clearer and clearer that whilst under certain circumstances the one may be more capable and the other less – the spirit remains a reality in its own right.

People picture an abstraction when they speak of 'free spirit', but that is simply not a reality. The free spirit is something which really lives among human beings, only one must allow it to come into existence. It works amongst human beings only it must be allowed to come into existence!

What I have said to you today I have said primarily in order that we may reap the benefits which can flow from principal feelings, from feelings for the seriousness of the matter.

I am of course not of the opinion that now everyone will immediately go out and speak well, in the same way as the ancients spoke beautifully, and those in between spoke correctly!

But you cannot therefore raise the objection: What good then is all our lecturing if we cannot immediately speak well? It all depends on our really acquiring a feeling for the earnestness of the situation into which we have to find our way. We shall have to acknowledge that what is required is something so organically whole, that little by little a necessity of form

198

corresponding to that of the whole human being is expressed in the lobe of the ear – that and no other.

So I will try to draw still closer together the content of Anthroposophy and the Threefold Social Order with the method in which it should be presented, and from the principles I shall approach ever more and more the concrete and that which should lie at the basis of practice.

*

What then must the preparation for a talk be?

Well, one should try to enter into the situation or into that for which the audience is prepared, by forming the first sentences in the way in which one deems fit. It will be necessary to take greater pains in speaking to an unprepared audience than will be the case when speaking to a circle of people who are already acquainted with the subject, at least as far as their feelings are concerned.

The rest of the talk need not be written down, nor need one jot down mere headings. Experience shows that writing it down word for word leads just as little to a good talk, as the jotting down of headings. Do not write it down; because it thereby binds you, and can lead to embarrassment if memory fails you. That is very likely to happen when a talk is written down word for word. Short headings easily lead to the preparation of the talk becoming too abstract in form. It is best to write down, and even to bring the document along with you if you need to have something of the sort, a series of properly-formulated sentences as title-sentences, which do not need to be spoken as part of the talk, but which are simply there: firstly, secondly, thirdly, etc., and which give in a way a kind of extract, so that perhaps ten or eight, or twelve sentences can grow out of each one. But these sentences must be written down. Do not write down for instance: 'Spirit life as independent', but: 'Spiritual Life can only thrive when it works from out of itself independently'. So – sentences as headings. When you do something of this kind you yourself will have the experience, in a comparatively short time, of entering into a certain possibility of free speaking, assisted only by the step-ladder of the written sentences.

At the end, it is often very good if we gently refer back again to the beginning – if the end has something that was already there as motif at the beginning.

By writing these sentences down on paper you give yourself the possibility of preparing yourself for your talk in the way I have previously indicated. So now consider: What you have to say about the spiritual life must assume a lyrical character within you. What you have to say about the life of rights must assume a kind of dramatic character within you, and what you have to say about the economic life must assume a narrative-epic character within you, a calm narrative-epic quality. Then in fact, instinctively, the longing will begin to arise, and the art will also begin to arise of cultivating, in the formulation of these sentences, something in the nature of that of which I have been speaking. Purely through the feelings, the preparation will proceed in such a way that in fact one's way of speaking will grow into what has to be said by way of content.

But for this it is of course essential that to a certain extent the control of one's speech has become instinct. The speech organs must be felt in a way similar to that in which a hammer is felt when we want to do something with it. This can be achieved by practising speech gymnastic exercises. You see, when you practise gymnastic exercises, they are not movements which are carried out in everyday life, but movements which make you supple and skilful. And in the same way the organs of speech should be made supple and flexible, but so that this making flexible is connected with the inner life of soul. Then one learns to feel the sounds in speaking. In the training course which I held more than two years ago for the Waldorf teachers in Stuttgart, I composed a series of such speech exercises, which I would like to give to you now.* They are of such a nature that their content seldom prevents you from entering purely into the element of speech. They simply aim at practising gymnastics in speech. These exercises should be spoken out loud over and

* See pp. 46 ff.

over again in such a way that you probe how best to use your tongue and your lips to produce a particular succession of sounds. You thus make yourself independent of speech itself and can then concentrate more on the mental preparation for your talk.

I shall read you a series of such exercises. They are often meaningless as regards content, but they are intended to make the organs of speech supple for the purposes of lecturing.

Dass er dir log uns darf es nicht loben
Dart may these boats through darkening gloaming

is the simplest. A more complicated one is:

Nimm nicht Nonnen in nimmermüde Mühlen
Name neat Norman on nimble moody mules

Another example:

Rate mir mehrere Rätsel nur richtig
Rattle me more and more rattles now rightly

It is of course not enough to say something of this kind once or even ten times, but over and over again, because even if the organs of speech are already flexible, they can become more so.

An example which I believe to be quite especially useful is the following:

Redlich ratsam	Rateless ration
Rüstet rühmlich	roosted roomily
Riesig rächend	reason wretched
Ruhig rollend	ruined Roland
Reuige Rosse	royalty roster

In this case one has at the same time the opportunity of regulating the breath between the lines. Attention must be paid to this as it can be practised especially well through such an exercise.

In the same kind of way – all sounds are not of equal value for these gymnastics – you will make progress if you practise the following:

Protzig preist	Proxy prized
Bäder brünstig	bather broomstick
Polternd putzig	polka pushing
Bieder bastelnd	beady basket
Puder patzend	prudent pertness
Bergig brüstend	bearskin bristled

You will benefit greatly if you are successful in finding your way gradually into this succession of sounds.

When you have done such exercises as these you could also try to do those exercises which of necessity include bringing mood into the speaking of the sounds. I have tried to give in the following exercise an example of how the sound element can be poured into the mood:

Erfüllung geht	Fulfilling goes
Durch Hoffnung	Through hoping
Geht durch sehnen	Goes through longing
Durch wollen	Through willing

and now it comes more into the sounding, and the mood is held in the sounds themselves.

Wollen weht	Willing flows
Im Webenden	In wavering
Weht im Bebenden	Wails in quavering
Webt bebend	Waves veiling
Webend bindend	Waving breathing
Im Finden	In freedom
Findend windend	Freedom winning
Kündend	Kindling

You will always find, when you do these exercises, that you are in a position to regulate your breath without the breath disturbing you, if you simply keep to the sounds. All kinds of clever methods have recently been thought out in connection with breathing, and every other possible phenomenon accompanying speaking and singing, but they are all useless. For speaking, with all that pertains to it, including the breathing, should be learnt from speaking itself. That means that one must learn to speak in such a way that in the necessities presented by the succession of sounds, the word-order, the breath, too, is regulated as a matter of course. *Only through speaking itself should breathing for speaking be learnt.* The speech exercises should be so, that one is compelled through this correct feeling for the sounds – not for the content but for the sounds – compelled through this correct feeling for the sounds to regulate the breath.

The following verse is concerned with mood derived from the content. It has four lines. These four lines are arranged in such a way that they are in a sense an intensification. Each line arouses expectation, while the fifth line is the conclusion, and brings fulfilment. One should really try to carry out this *speech movement* that I have just characterized. The verse is:

> *In den unermesslich weiten Räumen,*
> *In den endenlosen Zeiten,*
> *In der Menschenseele Tiefen,*
> *In der Welten Offenbarung:*
> *Suche des grossen Rätsels Lösung.*

> In the vast unmeasured worldwide spaces,
> In the endless stream of time,
> In the depths of human soul-life,
> In the world's great revelations:
> Seek the unfolding of life's great mystery.

Here you have the fifth line as the fulfilment of that gradual expectation suggested in the first four lines.

Now, you can also try to bring the mood of the situation into the very sounding of the words, into the very way of speaking. And for this purpose I have formed the following exercise. Picture to yourself a really big green frog which sits in front of you with its mouth open – there it is sitting, a gigantic frog with its mouth open. Now imagine what kind of emotions you might have when facing this frog. You will probably experience humour, and perhaps certain other things too. Conjure this up really vividly in your soul, then speak to the frog in this way:

Lalle Lieder lieblich	Lulling leader limply
Lipplicher Laffe	liplessly laughing
Lappiger lumpiger	loppety lumpety
Laichiger Lurch	lackety lout

Picture a field with a horse running over it. The content is not important. Now of course you must imagine that horses whistle. Now give utterance to this fact in the following way:

Pfiffig pfeifen	Piffling fifer
Pfäffische Pferde	prefacing feather
Pflegend Pflüge	phlegma fluting
Pferchend Pfirsiche	fairground piercing

Then make a variation by saying it in this way:

Pfiffig pfeifen aus Näpfen
Pfäffische Pferde schlüpfend
Pflegend Pflüge hüpfend
Pferchend Pfirsiche knüpfend

Please learn it by heart, so that you can say the one form and then the other following it very fluently. Then there is yet a third form. Learn all three by heart and try to speak them so fluently that you never confuse the one with the other. That is what matters here. Take as the third form:

Kopfpfiffig pfeifen aus Näpfen
Napfpfäffische Pferde schlüpfend
Wipfend pflegend Pflüge hüpfend
Tipfend pferchend Pfirsiche knüpfend

Practise all three one after the other when you know them by heart, so that one form never disturbs you whilst you are speaking another. You can do something similar with the two following exercises.

204

Ketzer petzten jetzt kläglich	Curtsey Betsy jets cleric
Letzlich leicht skeptisch	Lastly light sceptic

and now the other form:

Ketzer krächzer petzten jetzt kläglich
Letzlich plötzlich leicht skeptisch

Curtsey cressets Betsy jets cleric
Lastly plotless light sceptic

Again, learn them by heart and say them one after the other!
Your speech will become flexible if you practise something like
the following:

Nur renn	Narrow wren
Nimmer reuig	mirror royal
Gierig grinsend	gearing grizzled
Knoten knipsend	noting nippers
Pfänder knüpfend	fender coughing

One must accustom oneself to saying this succession of sounds.
You will see what it does for your tongue and all your organs of
speech if you do exercises such as this.

Now one that takes somewhat longer, an exercise of a kind
that produces flexibility. I believe that even actors have discovered after practising this exercise that it is the best of all for
making their speech flexible:

Zuwider zwingen zwar	Tu-whit twinkle 'twas
Zweizweckige Zwacker zu wenig	Twice twigged tweaker to twenty
Zwanzig Zwerge	Twangy twirlings
Die sehnige Krebse	The zinnia crisper
Sicher suchend schmausen	Zither zooming shambles
Dass schmatzende Schmachter	This smartened
Schmiegsam schnellstens	Smacking smuggler
Schnurrig schnaltzen	Sneezing snoring snatching

Then now and again one needs presence of mind whilst speaking, and can cultivate it through the following:

205

Klipp plapp plick glick	Clip plop pluck cluck
Klingt Klapper richtig	Clinked clapper richly
Knatternd trappend	Knotted trappings
Rossegetrampel	Rosily tripled

Then, for still more presence of mind, the two following examples which can be taken together:

Schlinge Schlange geschwinde	Slinging slanging a swindler
Gewundene Fundewecken weg	The wounding fooled a victor vexed

Then the same sound-motif in this way:

Gewundene Fundewecken	The wounding fooled a swindler
Geschwinde schlinge Schlange weg	Slinging slanging vexed

The *Wecken weg* is also in this one. Then, to strengthen your speech so that you can bowl someone over now and again in a discussion (this is necessary sometimes in speech) the following example:

Marsh schmachtender	March smarten ten
Klappriger Racker	claprigging rockets
Krackle plappernd linkisch	crackling plopping lynxes
Flink von vorne fort	Fling from forward forth

Then, in addition, for someone inclined to stammer, the following exercises should be introduced:

Nimm mir nimmer
Was sich wässerig
Mit Teilen mitteilt

This is good for every stammerer. The following can also be used:

Nimmer nimm mir
Wässerige Wickel
Was sich schlecht mitteilt
Mit Teilen deiner Rede

It all depends, of course, on the stammerer himself taking pains.

One should really not believe that one can, or should, only practise what I would call speech gymnastics with sentences meaningful to the intellect. In such sentences the attention is drawn unconsciously and instinctively too strongly to the sense, for the sounds to be properly considered. And it is even necessary, if we want to lecture, to pay attention also to the fact that we must set speech free in a certain sense from ourselves, really set it free. Yes, just as one can set writing free from oneself one can set speech free from oneself.

There are two ways of writing. The one way consists in a person writing egoistically – having the forms of the letters in his limbs so to speak, and allowing them to flow out of his limbs. This kind of writing was rated very highly for a time. It may even be that this is still the case when instruction in writing is given to business people and the like. I once watched for instance how writing instruction of this kind was given to some clerks. It was done in such a way that every letter had to be developed out of a kind of curve. They had to learn to swing their hand, then bring it down on the paper. Everything was in the hand, in the limb, so that actually only the hand was used in writing. Another kind of writing is the non-egoistic, the selfless way of writing. It consists in not writing with the hand but with the eye, so that one, basically speaking, draws the letters, and the joints of the hand are of little importance. One actually proceeds as one does in drawing. One is not the slave of one's handwriting, but one comes gradually to the point where one even has trouble writing one's name in the way one has hitherto written it. For most people it is so terribly easy to write their name in the way they have hitherto written it. It simply comes out of their hand.

But the people who put something artistic into their script, write with their eye. They follow through the stroke of their pen with their eye. The script is in fact separated from the human being. Then a person can – but it is not desirable in a certain respect to practise this – imitate other people's handwriting, vary their script in different ways. I am not saying that one ought to practise this particularly, but I do say that it appears as an extreme when one 'paints' the handwriting. That is the selfless way of writing; writing out of the limbs, on the other hand, is the selfish, the egoistic way of writing.

With most people speech also is egoistic, but you can gradually accustom yourself to experience your speech as if it actually wafted around you, as if the words moved in the air around you. You can really have a kind of sensing of your words. Then speech is separated off from the human being. It becomes objective. Man quite instinctively hears himself speaking. His head becomes, as it were, bigger, and he feels the weaving of the sounds and of the words around him. He learns gradually to listen to the sounds, to the words. This is precisely what can be achieved through exercises of the kind I have given you.

It is not merely a case of shouting into space – and by shouting I do not mean simply yelling, since it is also possible to shout in a whisper when one is speaking to oneself, just letting it come straight from the speech organs – but one lives in speaking really with space. One feels the resonance, as it were, in space. In certain theories of speech, theories connected with the teaching or learning of speech, if you will, this has recently become an absolute nonsense, because they speak with body resonance, stomach resonance, nasal resonance and so on. But this is all nonsense. A real resonance can only be one that is experienced, for instance, not in the sound striking against the interior of the nose, but in front of the nose, outside. So that speech in reality acquires a fullness. Altogether speech should have fullness and the speaker should swallow the words as little as possible. Do not believe that this is of no significance for the speaker. On the contrary, it is of the greatest significance, for whether we are able to present something to people in the right way or not depends entirely upon our relationship to speech itself. It is not necessary to go as far as an actor friend of mine, who never said *friend*ship, but always *friendship*, because he wanted to lay stress on every syllable. He took it to extremes. But one should develop the instinctive ability not to swallow syllables in any shape or form. This can be done by trying to find one's way into rhythmical language, speaking it in such a way that one goes into the whole shape and form of the sounds.

Und es wallet und siedet und brauset und zischt,
Wie wenn Wasser mit Feuer sich mengt.

So: do not only go into the sounds as such, but also into their shape and form – into their round or angular nature.

If anyone believes he can become a speaker without appreciating the value of this, he is making the same kind of mistake as does a human soul, who, in the life between death and rebirth, has reached the point of descending to earth, but does not want to embody, because it does not want to enter into the formation of stomach, lungs, kidneys, and so on. Everything has to be taken into account which has to be introduced into one's speaking, which actually gives finished form to one's lecturing.

And so it is necessary to appreciate the value of the organism of speech and its genius. One should not forget that this appreciation of the organism of speech, of the genius of speech, is pictorially creative. He who is not engaged with speech, hearing inwardly – to him come no pictures and no thoughts. He remains clumsy in his thinking, and abstract, if not pedantic, in his speaking. It is just by experiencing the nature of the sounds, the pictorial element in the forming of speech itself, that something lies which conjures out of our souls even the very thoughts we require to present to our audience. In the experiencing of the word lies something creative in relation to our inner being which should never be overlooked. This is extraordinarily important. We ought actually to be ruled by the feeling for how the word, the sequence of words, the formation of words and the formation of sentences are connected with our whole organization. Just as we can solve, in a certain way, the riddle of man from his physiognomy, so can we feel even more what the whole person is like from the way in which he speaks, – not what he says, but how he says it.

This way of speaking comes out of the whole human being.

And it is also important to keep the physical body in mind, in a gentle sort of way – not treating it as a patient, of course, but in a mild, gentle way. It is good, for instance, for someone who is inclined, whether through education or heredity, to speak pedantically, to try to overcome his pedantry through the occasional drinking of a stimulating tea. However, as I said before, these things must be done with care. One tea is good for one person, another for another. Ordinary tea is, as I have often mentioned, a very good beverage for diplomats. Diplomats have to be brilliant and witty, rattling off one thing after another without any continuity. They shouldn't be pedantic on any account, but must demonstrate an easy transition from one subject to another. Therefore tea is the drink for diplomats. Coffee makes one logical. That's why journalists very often write their articles in coffee houses, because they are not usually by nature very logical. Now, of course, in the age of the typewriter, things are rather different. However, previously one could meet whole troups of journalists in coffee houses gnawing their pens, and drinking coffee, in order that one thought should follow on after the other. So if you find you have too much of a tea nature, coffee can even it out. But, as I have already said, this is not really to be regarded as medication, though it lies nonetheless in that direction. And if someone is inclined to obtrude the sound E (eh) or something of the sort into his speech after every third syllable or so, I would advise him to drink weak senna-leaf tea twice a week in the evening, and see what a beneficial effect it has.

The things that come to expression in speech must surely come out of the whole human being, and therefore diet cannot be ignored. I do not mean this only in the coarser sense. If a person has poured endless quantities of beer down his throat, it can obviously be heard in his speech. Those who have an ear for speech know quite well whether a speaker is a tea drinker or a coffee drinker; whether he suffers from constipation or the opposite. In speech everything comes to expression with absolute exactitude, and attention must be paid to this. It is possible to enter gradually into these things quite instinctively when one feels speech in one's surrounding.

It is certainly true that the different languages incline in different ways and in different degrees to being heard in the surrounding in this way. A language like Latin is specially suited to being heard in this way. Italian too. (I mean now to being heard by the speaker himself as something objective.) The English language, for instance, is little suited to this, because, as language, it is too similar to the writing that flows out of the limbs. The more abstract languages become, the less suited they are to being heard inwardly, to becoming objective. How the German *Nibelungenlied* rang in ancient times.

> *Uns ist in alten mæren   wunders vil geseit*
> *Von heleden lobebæren,   von grôzer arebeit*

That rings! From things such as these one must learn to experience speech. Languages become abstract by nature during the course of their development. Then the concrete element, the sense-perceptible element must be introduced more from within.

Placed abstractly beside each other, what a difference there is:

> *Uns ist in alten mæren   wunders vil geseit*

and

> *Uns wird in alten Märchen   Wunderbares viel erzählt*

It can, of course, also be introduced into the more modern languages, when one has accustomed oneself to hearing in this way. A lot can be done in speech so that it becomes something that has its own genius. Exercises such as these are required in order to link up hearing in the spirit and speaking out of the spirit, and in this connection I will give once again the exercise:

> *Erfüllung geht*   Fulfilling goes
> *Durch Hoffnung*   Through hoping
> *Geht durch Sehnen*   Goes through longing
> *Durch Wollen*   Through willing

Wollen weht	Willing flows
Im Webenden	In wavering
Weht im Bebenden	Wails in quavering
Webt bebend	Waves veiling
Webend bindend	Waving breathing
Im Finden	In freedom
Findend windend	Freedom winning
Kündend	Kindling

Only by placing a particular sound in a variety of contexts does one arrive at the sensing of the sound, at the metamorphosis of the sound, and at the viewing of the word, the looking at the word. When something akin to what I have demonstrated to you today by way of mental preparation through the title-sentences is united with what we can acquire from speech itself, then we can go on to the question of lecturing.

There is one more thing that is needed for lecturing, apart from all the other things I have mentioned, and that is a sense of responsibility. That means, one should feel that one has no right to parade all one's speech defects before an audience. One should learn to feel that one needs a training in speech, a going out beyond oneself and a plastic modelling of one's speech when addressing an audience. Responsibility towards speech. . . . It is of course more comfortable to stick where you are, to speak as you usually speak, to swallow what you usually swallow, to squeeze and chop and cut and press and drawl the words just as it suits you. But there is no need to keep on squeezing and pressing and drawing one's words and so on. One must try to assist one's speech, even in these matters of form.

When assistance is given to your speech in this way, you will be led to speak in public with a certain sense of respect, to approach such speaking with a certain feeling of awe. This is absolutely necessary and it can be achieved by working out the mental aspect on the one hand, and the more physical aspect which I have presented in the second part today, on the other. Even if your lecture is merely informal, things such as these must be taken very much into account. Let us say, for example, you have to speak about the Goetheanum. Fundamentally speaking, you cannot make a special preparation for every occasion, but at least twice a week you should prepare yourself in the way I have described. One should only speak extempore when one is in continual practise.

Then you will also find how the formal element unites with the content. And it is just on this point that we shall have more to say tomorrow, on the connecting-up of formal practice with mental practice.

*

The artistic element is something that must be taken into account when lecturing, the more so as one has to pay attention to logic, to day-to-day experience, and to other powers of understanding. It is probably all the more necessary to proceed artistically by means of repetition, composition and certain other factors to be mentioned today, the more one has to appeal to the understanding through a stringent application of thought.

It is important to know that the artistic element itself offers a means of understanding. Repetition as such, for instance, works in such a way that it facilitates hearing. It gives the listener the opportunity of not holding strictly to the one or other phrase, but to that which lies in between. In this way his power of comprehension is set free. And this feeling of being freed is something that makes an extraordinary contribution towards understanding.

But other means also should be applied; not only those of artistic construction, but of artistic execution. For instance, the speaker should introduce questions from time to time, addressing his audience directly with a question in between his other statements. What does it mean to address one's audience with a question? Well, questions work chiefly on the inhalation of the listener. The audience, whilst listening, lives in the process of inhalation and exhalation. Inhalation – exhalation is of importance not only for the speaker but for the listener as well.

If a speaker introduces a question, exhalation is held as it were in suspension. Inhalation is absorbed by the listening when a question is heard. It is no contradiction if the speaker poses his question just as the listener is breathing out. One listens not only directly, but obliquely, so that the actual hearing of a word or sentence which coincides with an exhalation is only really perceived during the following inhalation, if it has been a question. In short, inhalation has, on the whole, essentially to do with what is posed in the form of a question, but through the engagement of the inhalation in the posing of the question, the whole process of listening is internalized. It proceeds, as it were, at a deeper level of the soul than is the case when one is merely listening to statements. One always has the tendency, when listening to statements, of being engaged neither with one's inhalation nor one's exhalation. The statement does not want to go any deeper than necessary, neither does it want to engage the sense-organs.

The oral explanation of logical matters is, on the whole, an awkward business. Those who wish to speak in such a way that they merely present a set of finished conclusions to their audience, have an excellent means of sending them off to sleep, for this development of logic has the disadvantage of removing understanding from the organ of hearing. One does not listen properly to what is logical, and, on the other hand, it does not give proper shape and form to the breathing. Logic does not set it moving in varied waves. The breath actually remains most neutral when listening to logical statements, and it is for this reason that they send you to sleep. That is a completely organic process. Logical utterances wish to be impersonal, but that takes its revenge. Therefore, if one wishes to develop into a good speaker, one must take care wherever possible, in spite of remaining logical, to speak not merely in logical formulae, but rather in figures of speech, amongst which we have the question.

In this respect, an enormous amount could be said about the forming of a lecture. One normally believes that people hear merely with their ears, but there is something that contradicts this. Some people, particularly when they want to grasp something, open their mouths when listening. They would not do this if they heard merely with their ears.

One listens far more with the organs of speech than one generally believes. In a manner of speaking one is always engaged in the speaker's talk, with one's organs of speech, and the ether body always speaks, too, always does eurythmy whilst listening. The movements conform absolutely to the movements of eurythmy, but usually one is unaware of this if one has not learnt eurythmy.

It is so that everything heard from inorganic bodies is heard with the ear from outside, but the speech of man is heard in such a way that one becomes aware of what strikes the ear from inside. That is a fact. Very few people know what a great difference exists between the hearing of the sound of a bell, or of a symphony, and the hearing of human speech. With human speech it is actually the accompanying inner speaking that is heard. This is much more of an accompanying phenomenon than it is when one is listening to the sound of something inorganic. For that reason I had to say what I did about one's own listening so that the lecture is formulated in the way in which one would criticize it if one heard it. I mean that the formulation must come from the same force, from the same impulse, as criticism, if one is listening.

It will be of some importance if those who make it their task to work for the Threefold Social Organism or something similar, take care to present what they have to say to the public in a manner that is also artistic.

ON SPEECH DEFECTS

I think we could discuss today questions that one or other of our esteemed listeners may raise in connection with what has been developed here as Anthroposophy during the last few days. It is not possible to touch on the one theme or the other even sketchily, although there will be well-nigh a hundred lectures during the course of these three weeks, as I tried to convey today, but only an impulse can be given for the time being – an impulse, however, which will perhaps show that the anthroposophically oriented Spiritual Science we have in mind here is just as well-grounded as that which is accepted in external life as contemporary exact science. It takes up into itself all the methodic discipline of this science and also perceives precisely what exists as a great demand of our age for further development. It stands as a great demand for further development precisely because those impulses, especially of scientific life, that produced greatness in the epoch just ended, are in the process of dying away today and would lead to the decline of humanity, to the decline of our civilization, were a new impulse not to come. The suggestions given for a new impulse of this kind can certainly be enlarged upon in various ways in a discussion such as this. For such amplification I would crave your assistance, and ask you to put questions, express wishes, and simply introduce what you want to introduce. The questions are best put in writing, and I would ask you to make good use of the opportunity.

A participant: The question I have to put is related to a therapeutic sphere. Dr. Steiner in his lectures has pointed to certain illnesses of our time that frequently make their appearance these days. There are certain mental disturbances and I would be grateful for a reply concerning their deeper origins. It is a matter chiefly of speech disturbances. I would remark that in the answer my personal interests should only play a part in so far as they are of general pedagogical interest. I have been asked by teachers what should be done in the case of speech disturbances. With this question, which enters into the therapeutic sphere, I do not wish to stimulate questions that concern only illness. I would be very grateful for an answer, because it seems to me to be a burning question at present.

Dr. Steiner: We can perhaps make a start by answering this question. One must, when something special of this nature is asked, of course consider the fact that particular disturbances of this kind in the human organism can have the most varied origins. When one wants to go into the true cause it is exceptionally difficult to speak about these things in general terms. In such instances it actually depends upon our putting ourselves in a position, through Spiritual Science, of judging the particular case in the right way. And for this reason I would like to say something that perhaps has a more general significance than the question itself calls for.

You see, we live in an age of abstraction, in an age when one loves to reduce the manifold world, the multiform world, to a few formulae, when one loves to draw up abstract laws embracing vast fields of experience. You can then only embrace them in an abstract way, by leaving out everything individual. Spiritual Science will have to bring about a significant change in this respect. It will revel less in the simplifications of manifold existence but will bring knowledge to bear on the concrete spiritual. Through approaching the concrete spiritual, one is so stimulated in one's whole mental attitude that the capacity to observe, the capacity to judge and the capacity to inspire are all strengthened and reinforced. That will become apparent, I would say, in general social intercourse. A large part of our social question today lies in our no longer having any inclination to get to know the people who pass us by. We no longer have the inner impulse that makes it possible to grasp what is individual, particular. In this respect Spiritual Science will create something different. It will make our inner life rich again and will make us capable of entering into the particular. In this way such things as the capacity for observation and the capacity for differentiation will be especially cultivated. Then we shall have less pleasure in abstract generalizations and more pleasure in detail, in the singular. We shall, in a way, keep more to the example than to the abstraction. Especially in dealing with something in the nature of physical disturbances, speech disturbances, it is necessary to say that almost every single case – that is of course somewhat exaggerated, but valid generally – almost every single case is different, and one must at least differentiate between types.

We must be clear about the fact that a part of what produces speech impediments is of course organically determined, which means that it rests in a certain way on the defective development of one organ or another, but a whole series of such impediments at present certainly comes from the fact that the powers of soul and spirit in man are not developed in the right way. It may even be said that if a correct development of the human faculties of soul and spirit can be attained through education in childhood, while the human organism is still flexible, organic disturbances can also be overcome to a certain degree, certainly more easily than at a later stage when the body has become more hardened.

The whole nature of our education has basically become a business in abstraction. Our education does not suffer from bad principles, because generally speaking, if we would look at the abstract treatment of pedagogical principles, we can boast of great and significant achievements during the last century.

If you look at the abstract methods of application concerning how to do this or that in school, one would have to say that in this respect the pedagogy of the nineteenth century really signified something tremendous. But it is just the art of taking an interest in each single child, of noticing the special development of each single child, that has been lost in recent times through the race towards intellectuality and abstractness. Through abstract pedagogy we are, in a way, no longer able to strengthen the soul and spirit element in the child in the right way. Do not imagine that in saying this we would point in a one-sided way to an education in soul and spirit estranged from the world. Oh no! it may seem paradoxical but it is in fact the case that materialism has had the tragic destiny that it has not been able to master material phenomena. The best example of this is that we have such psychological theories as psycho-somatic parallelism. On the one hand there is human corporeality, known only through an anatomy learned primarily from the corpse, and on the other hand, we have thought-out, or even only verbal theories, concerning soul and spirit. And then one goes on to think about how this soul and spirit, which has no similarity with the corporeal body, could affect this body.

Spiritual Science will lead to our being able to penetrate concretely again into the bodily aspect, and to our knowing once again such things as I have already indicated in the lecture,* the importance of which I should like to mention again here. As human beings, something is at work in us from birth to the change of teeth which we could call a sum total of forces of equilibrium, which organize us, through and through, something in the nature of forces of movement, life forces.† These work particularly strongly in our organism during this time. What works in man then thrusts out the second teeth – it comes to a conclusion with the thrusting out of the second teeth. In a way it ends its activity to a certain degree – although there is of course a continuation – when the second teeth appear.

It is then changed into what we could call mathematical geometrical thinking, what we could call thinking about the states of equilibrium in space, thinking about the relationships of movement in space, what we could call relating ourselves to conditions of life in space and time. That which emerges which goes over from a latent to a freed state is what we study when it has become free. We have it then as something of soul and spirit, as something quite concrete in soul and spirit. We see it growing in the child when the change of teeth begins, and on into the later years of life. Looking at it we see what is of the nature of soul and spirit working in an organizing capacity in the body in the first seven years of life.

We can study yet another relationship of soul and spirit with the physical organization if we bear in mind what man experiences – albeit consciously only in Inspiration – with his ordinary consciousness, but 'unconsciously' during the time between the change of teeth and puberty. It is more a dipping down into the physical corporeality, where during the course of events, it arouses, as its main phenomenon – though there are others – the urge to love. This reaches its conclusion in the male with the alteration of the voice, and in the female with somewhat more diffuse but nonetheless discernible effects. That, again, which we recognize when we regard the development of the

* See Rudolf Steiner, *Grenzen der Naturerkenntnis*, Rudolf Steiner Nachlassverwaltung, Dornach, 1969.
† See also: Rudolf Steiner, *Theosophy*, Rudolf Steiner Press, London, 1973 and *Occult Science – An Outline*, Rudolf Steiner Press, London, 1969.

world of feeling, particularly something like the development of the sense for music, just at the time when the world of feeling is developing – we study this again as the connection of soul and spirit with the physical organization from the seventh to the fourteenth or fifteenth year. In short, Spiritual Science does not pose the abstract question 'How does the soul work upon the body?' Spiritual Science studies the concrete element of soul, but it knows that it must look at this concrete element of soul at a certain time of life, and that at another time of life it works upon the body. It changes the abstract and unsatisfactory methods of treatment in contemporary psychology and physiology to absolutely concrete methods. In course of time one comes to the point where one cannot assert in general through Spiritual Science that during the first seven years the power of balance, the power of motion, and the power of life are working, but one is enabled to specialize by beholding the spiritual element concretely, learning to see how this spiritual element is expressed in the organs, how this spiritual element works in the lungs, the heart and liver, and so on. One acquires the possibility of looking into the human body in a really living way. Then something quite different emerges from what the knowledge of matter, from what materialism can produce. The special feature of materialism is that it yields to a false, that is to say, an abstract, an abstracted spirituality. The special feature of Spiritual Science is that it will be able to judge even the material factor in the right way. Of course on the other hand, it also leads towards the spiritual in the right way. Actually one should combat ever more vigorously the opinions emanating from nebulous mystics to the effect that Spiritual Science is something that takes an interest in fantasms, generalities, and empty talk. No, Spiritual Science goes into the concrete factor and would show how the elements of soul and spirit work right into the several organs. For one can only acknowledge material existence by getting to know the working of the spirit in a concrete way in material existence. It is especially through such concrete penetration into the human organism that one gradually acquires – because one only acquires something of this sort through a kind of Imagination, Inspiration and so on – one gradually acquires a capacity, I would say, a gift, for really seeing what is individual, and then for being able to judge where the particular fault lies in the case of speech disturbance, for instance. Then it will be possible to work with special speech exercises on the development of the speech organs at a certain age in childhood. It all depends on noticing at the right age, on observing what physical disturbances there are. Although we are prevented simply by external circumstances – one only acknowledges nowadays and allows to carry on in practice what bears an official stamp in this direction – although every possible hindrance is placed in the way, we can, nonetheless say, for example, that particularly in respect of speech impediments good results have been attained with rhythmic speech exercises. One recognizes the particular fault, and makes the person with the faulty speech organism recite something repeatedly in one speech rhythm or another, pointing out to him the need to enter with special feeling into the rhythmic progression of the sounds. In this way one can bring some relief in respect of such disturbances.*

But something else is also possible. One can, for instance, in the case of speech disturbances work especially on the control of the breath process, but of course, in a quite individual way. This control of the process of breathing can be achieved by allowing the person one is treating to develop a feeling for saying inwardly, or perhaps only thinking – a fast or slow thinking – a certain series of words or thoughts. The peculiar thing is that when one forms such series of words in the right way, and surrenders oneself to a thought rhythm, or inner word rhythm of this kind, one transfers the feeling to the person being treated that with such a saying, in a faster or slower tempo, you can notice a change in your breathing. The breathing alters in one way or another. You follow this and bring to consciousness in a certain way what appears as parallel phenomenon in the breath

---

* Compare the observations on pp. 156 ff. Also Rudolf Steiner, *Erneuerung der pädagogischen Kunst durch Geisteswissenschaft*, Lecture XII, Rudolf Steiner Verlag, Dornach, 1958.

to the inward picturing or imagining of speech. When the person you are treating is able to inform you of this, you can go on trying to help him, so that once he has brought his breathing process to consciousness, he gradually reaches the point where he himself can make up his own series of words to correspond with his breathing process, which he is now able, in a certain way, to follow consciously.

So, one has to think of the matter in this way by giving rhythms to begin with, which, according to the situation, have to be inwardly thought, murmured, whispered, or said aloud, one summons up in the person concerned attention to the alteration in his breathing. Now he knows: the breathing is altered in this way. And then, one forbids him in a certain sense to use that very material in thought and word that one has given him. One draw his attention to the fact that he should now make within himself something similar. Then he comes to the point of introducing a conscious parallelism of this process of inner thought and word, this inner process of hearing words, with the process of breathing. So that a certain breathing always corresponds with an inner picturing or inner hearing of words. In this way, a great deal is evened out concerning what I would call bad association between the processes which are more of a mental nature, inclining more toward the soul when one speaks, and those processes which run their course in the organism more as material, physical processes. All this works particularly beneficially when one applies it at the correct age in childhood. One could even say that if our educationalists were better psychologists, and if they really had a concrete knowledge of the human body out of the spirit, they would be able to work in quite a different way educationally in the realm of speech impediments.

One can, of course, build up what I have said into a certain therapy, and some very beneficial results will be attained, even for later stages of life. However, it also seems to me to be of particular importance – and we could point to certain results achieved in this direction – it seems to me to be of special importance that things such as these may well be healed through a particularly rational application of the principle of imitation. But then one must have a much more intimate subjective-objective knowledge of the whole human organism and its different parts.

You see, people speak to each other in ordinary life, but they notice very few, I would say, of the imponderable effects passing from one person to another in speaking. But these effects are nonetheless there. We have become so abstract today that we actually only listen to one another in respect of intellectual content. Very few people have a feeling today for what it actually means when a person equipped with a rather more psychic-organic sensibility feels, when he has spoken with someone, how he continues to bear the other person's manner of speaking in his own speech organism to a high degree, consciously. Very few people today have a feeling for all that one experiences in this direction when one has to speak with four, five or six people one after the other, of whom the first coughs, the second is hoarse, the third yells, and the fourth is incomprehensible. For your organism does it all as well. It goes on vibrating in sympathy, it experiences all that, too. In cultivating this feeling of sympathy in speech, though, one acquires a strong feeling also for self-protection. Then the strange thing emerges that one discovers from things as closely connected with the subjectivity of man as speech impediments the way to speak in front of such sufferers, the way to speak so that they achieve certain things through imitation, through copying. I have known stammerers achieve something like a forgetting of their stammering – I speak now comparatively – when one has been able to feel one's way into their disability and has then spoken for them something particularly rhythmically for them to repeat after one. It is essential to develop this feeling of human sympathy, right into his organic nature.

An enormous amount in the therapeutic realm depends on being able to forget the subjective experience connected with some objective process. A real remedy for speech disturbances, for example, is to make proper use of the time between the seventh and the fourteenth year, by gently bringing the sufferer to the kind of imitation I have described. One frequently encounters stammerers who cannot speak three words together without getting into difficulties, who cannot produce three words properly in succession.* If one gives them a poem to recite which they love and to which they can surrender themselves completely, and if one supports them as sympathetic listener, they can say quite a succession of verses without stammering. The fact that they are given the opportunity of doing something of this kind is in itself an especially good therapeutic medium, from the psychological point of view. One does harm to such people if one draws their attention to these failings by some external means. I had a friend who was also a poet, who could only express himself in a very explosive way when some tactless person drew attention to his stammering. Someone once asked him 'tactfully': 'Herr Doktor, do you always stammer like this?', and he replied 'No, only when I'm faced with someone I absolutely dislike' – I would, of course, have to stammer dreadfully if I had wanted to really imitate how he gave this answer.†

But now, it will gradually be recognized what a significant therapy we have for these and similar faults in the human organism, in eurythmy. This eurythmy can, I would say, be pursued in two directions. The one direction is that to which I have always drawn attention in the introductions‡ I give to the performances. I show there how, by looking at contemporary man by sensible-supersensible means, the speech organism becomes conscious in respect of its tendencies to movement, which are then transferred to the whole human organism. But the reverse direction is of no small significance. You have had presented to you today in a lecture from quite another viewpoint, the fact that without doubt a primordial human eurythmy most certainly played a significant role in the origins

* See pp. 159 ff.
† See Rudolf Steiner, *Speech and Drama*, Anthroposophical Publishing Company, London, 1960.
‡ See Rudolf Steiner, *Eurythmie als Impuls für künstlerisches Betätigen und Betrachten*, Dornach, 1954.

of speech. Things do not have their sound within them, as it were, in the sense of the ding-dong theory;* but there is a relationship between all things, between the whole macrocosm, and the human organization, this microcosm, and basically speaking all that happens in the external world is copied in a certain way in gesture and movement by the human organization.

So we have, fundamentally, the continuous tendency to reconstruct all phenomena through our own organism. We do not carry this out, however, with our physical organism, but with our etheric organism. The etheric organism is engaged in continuous eurythmy.

Primordial man was much more mobile than contemporary man. You know that this development from mobility to rest is still copied in certain circles. They regard it as a sign of education to behave as phlegmatically as possible when they speak, accompanying their speech with as few gestures as possible. Certain speakers regard it as 'respectable' always to have their hands in their trouser pockets so that they can make no gestures with their arms. It is judged to be the expression of a particularly good way of speaking if one stands there like a block of wood. But what comes to expression as a caricature in this case only corresponds to the progress of mankind from mobility to rest. In connection with human development we can ascertain that in times gone by a transition took place from a speaking in gesture, a kind of eurythmy, to a speaking in sounds. What has come to rest in the organism has settled especially in the organs of speech, and in the first place actually developed them. Just as the eye was made by the light so has the organ of speech been made by a speech that was once soundless. Once one knows all these connections, one will gradually be able to use eurythmy to very good advantage in teaching by introducing it correctly in order to counteract everything that might lead to a disturbance in speech. In this respect, it will be a very fascinating task, when you have a little spare time, to develop our present eurythmy, inclined as it is to the artistic and educational aspects ever more

* See p. 103.

and more in a therapeutic direction, and to build up a kind of curative eurythmy* which will cover such therapeutic demands as those mentioned here. I do not know whether what I have said is sufficient, but I just wanted to say a few words on the subject.

The 'conversation' was continued with questions on other subjects.

APHORISTIC REMARKS ON SPEECH FORMATION AND DRAMATIC ART†

I

Among the courses held in the Goetheanum during the first half of September was one on *Speech Formation and Dramatic Art.*‡ It was given to meet a quite definite need, felt by many people today, to get away from style-less naturalism on the stage and to get back to style again.

That will only be possible when one becomes aware at the very outset, of how the soul-content of man becomes manifest when it is given living shape in the word. As far as speaking is concerned, modern consciousness lives completely in the realm of the idea. It has almost lost the feeling for sound and word. In the realm of the idea, however, sense-perceptible spirituality, which is the essence of all art, is lost. Where dramatic art is concerned, this must be felt most of all, for it needs the element of mime, it needs the element of gesture, if it is to give the word its full value. Gesture does not connect itself so strongly with the feeling for the idea, as it does with the feeling for the sound and the word.

In making the sound A (ah) the soul always primarily reveals the experience of wonder at something, of amazement at

* See Rudolf Steiner, *Heileurythmie*, Rudolf Steiner Verlag, Dornach, 1966.
† These aphorisms summarize what Rudolf Steiner gave in the course on Speech Formation and Dramatic Art, the last in which he and Marie Steiner worked together.
‡ *Speech and Drama*, Rudolf Steiner, Anthroposophical Publishing Company, London, 1960.

something. In the sound O (oh) lives the feeling of the soul's surrounding of something. If one experiences language in this way, one finds in the making of the vowels the inner response of the soul to the outer world and in the making of the consonants the striving of the soul, through the very forming of the sounds, to create an audible image, in an imitative manner, of an object or process in the outer world.

One comes thereby to an experiencing of the Word.

In the b the soul strives to convey, in a process of imitation, the embracing of an object, and in the r, the inner agitation or trembling.

In the structure of vowels and consonants the life of the soul lives in the outer world, and the forms and processes of the outer world live as image in the soul.

In every word that contains the vowel A (ah) lives something of wonder or amazement in the soul towards a particular object. There is hardly a trace of this left for ordinary consciousness, but in the unconscious, or even the semi-conscious experiences of the human soul, the relationships of the human soul to the word exist. He who would reveal something artistically through the word must make these relationships alive within him. His soul must feel its way into the word, and only then can the word be formed artistically by him.

A dialogue presents what takes place between two people. Their souls interact. While the one speaks, the other listens. Then he begins to speak. In his words must reverberate what the first person experienced while he was speaking. He now listens to the other one. In his silent listening it must become evident for the dramatic presentation whether the second one pleases, disappoints, alarms or frightens him etc. For in art, everything that lives in it must be clearly presented.

The conduct of the two taking part in the dialogue results from the connections each has in his soul with the feeling for sound and word. Through this connection, the attitude the actor has to assume will become a matter of instinctive faculty.

Preparation for stage production should include a training of the feeling for sound and word.

The feeling for the idea cannot give any training appropriate to art, for it tends too strongly towards the intellect. This, however, destroys the artistic. It allows what is clearly visible to disappear into the invisibility of the inner life of the soul. What happens on the stage must live in the perceptibility of what is heard and what is seen. It must not need to be reconstrued by the intellect of those in the audience.

It was correctly thought by Aristotle, and correctly felt later by Lessing, that tragedy must re-echo in the fear and compassion of the onlooker. But these feelings will only be able to be kept alive through the actor if he can carry his life of soul right into his speech formation.

Life in speech can only be acquired by experiencing language. Nowadays one will naturally not always have words to speak which contain the U (oo) sound when one has to say something bearing an element of fear, for languages are no longer primordial. But the U (oo) sound is the manifestation of the experience of fear in the soul. If one has to say 'Danger is approaching' there is no U (oo) sound in it, but the intonation, which should be given to the words in this case can be cultivated from the feeling experienced in the sound U (oo).

It is the mystery of language that in every sound others resound with it inaudibly in the soul. If I speak A (ah) in a word that bears the element of fear, the U (oo) resounds with it in the depth of the soul. This of course, does not concern the person speaking in ordinary life. He stands within the immediate experience. He is close to the experience with his feeling. He speaks the words 'Danger is approaching' out of his experience of fear. The actor, however, does not stand directly in the actual situation, as in life. He must instinctively bear the feeling for sound within him, which then silently accompanies the words he has to utter to arouse fear. This feeling for the sound gives the intonation its right colouring.

A feeling of this kind for the sound will give the possibility in dialogue of the speakers answering each other in such a way that the interchange between the souls holding the conversation is made obvious to the onlooker. When one of the partners in a dialogue listens while the other speaks, the appropriate feeling for sound will vibrate within him, and as a result he will give his reply the correct intonation. A colour appears different depending on whether it is placed beside blue or beside yellow. A sentence, with whatever vowels, sounds differently depending on whether the fear-born U (oo) sound still vibrates with it, or the joy-borne I (ee) sound.

Marie Steiner and I are conducting this course jointly.

II

In dramatic art the inner life of speech must re-awaken, for a part of the human entity is contained in speech.

One finds this part when one seeks an understanding of the relationship of the element of mime, of the element of gesture, to the word. In the gesture lives a manifestation of the will of man imbued with feeling. The element of soul and spirit is present in the gesture as image. The element of soul and spirit allows the feeling to stream out into the pictoriality of the gesture, so the human being is revealed externally in the power of the will. One is engaged in making visible the human entity in such a way that the inner being is borne outwards.

But man can feel, can picture his own gesture, his own miming, just as he can picture things and processes of the outer world. In the picturing of the gesture there then lies a kind of filling of the consciousness with the inner human entity.

In ordinary life the human organization does not complete this transmission of the gesture borne by the will into the mental image. It checks it half way. And there where it is checked, speech arises. The elements of mime and gesture are embodied in the word. The word itself is a gesture in another form.

For the one who develops a feeling for the sound, it will become perceptible how the gesture slips into the sound, and in speaking he will have an experience of the gesture refined into the element of soul.

If one wants to shape speech artistically, one must be able to bear within oneself in this way the character of the word with the element of mime and gesture and only when the word is wrested free from the human throat, with the colouring of this experience, can it become the dramatic word.

In the dramatic word man in his movement must be made manifest through the sounds. Only then will a visible connection of gesture and mime with that which is spoken be made apparent to the eye and ear of the onlooker, and the drama will be able to flow through the actor's word and gesture.

What occurs in ordinary speaking in the human organism in the deeply hidden regions of the unconscious is the transformation of the mime and gesture into the intonation of the sound. That is what the actor must bring, through artistic feeling, to fantasy-filled consciousness. What the human being does ordinarily unconsciously in speaking, what in advanced languages has even vanished into a colourlessness of word-formation, must become in the actor the fantasy-conscious formation of the word. For this reason, the starting point in the actor's training must be the embodiment of the soul's experience in mime and gesture. This will only be possible with any measure of perfection if the prospective actor works at first together with a reciter, who does the speaking while he practises the role solely in mime and gesture, afterwards adding to this silent but eloquent practising, the colouring with the word.

Then the soul, which entrusts itself volitionally to the manifestation of movement, will also be able to live on the undulations of the word. For one experiences the soul in the engendering of the gesture, and in the word born of this gesture this experience is brought in to the more passive formation of the sounding element. If the actor finds his way into this connection between sound and the movement of the gesture, the shaping of the word will become fantasy-born instinct within him. This instinctive element must come into his experience, otherwise the presentation seems artificial. In order to be art, it must appear to have been born completely naturally.

One will only summon up enough will-force for the grasping of dramatic art in this way if one proceeds from a spiritual view of the human being. For a view of this kind will recognize in the lively speech of a person the weaving of the soul and spirit, and this can give the right basic mood for stage performance. Knowledge of man, transformation of the knowledge of man into the formation of sound and gesture in practice – that is the basis of dramatic art. What is inwardly experienced with one's whole being – the entrusting of oneself to the sound-accompanied gesture, to the gesture-accompanied word – that is the art of acting.

The above constitutes part of what was given in the course that has just been held at the Goetheanum on Speech Formation and Dramatic Art, which we hope will serve as a stimulus, a stimulus toward a renewal of the artistic on the stage. Marie Steiner has been developing the art of recitation and declamation for many years in such a way that in her the artistic element in speech formation has been raised to a living experience. We owe it to her that anthroposophical activity has been able to unfold in this direction. It is she who arranged for this course to take place, and she has also participated in it through her art of recitation. Through her encouragement a great number of actors have found their way here to the Goetheanum and under her guidance they have taken up into their dramatic art what Anthroposophy can give.

III

DECOR AND THE ART OF DIRECTION

The extracts that have so far been given here from the Speech and Drama Course should show how dramatic art has found its way to style from the direction of speech.

To produce a play on the stage the director has to enter into the world of colour. This applies to the costume of the players as well as to the stage setting. For the onlooker, what he hears as word, and sees as gesture, must be woven into a whole with the costumes of the actors and the moulding and painting of the scenery. Here it depends on the possibility of developing style in the colour gradations. For this reason, in dramatic art, as well as in painting, there must be an understanding for the transition which leads from the perception of the colour on the things and processes of the outer world, to the experience of the inner nature of colour.

A tragic mood on the stage, in a set keeping to reds or yellows, is impossible; and a cheerful frame of mind against a blue or deep violet background, equally so.

In colour, feeling lives in a spatial way. Just as the sight of red arouses a basic mood of the soul which is gay, of blue, one that is serious, and of violet, one that is ceremonious, so does the behaviour of one person towards another out of loving sacrifice require spatial embodiment in a costume which keeps to the reddish tones, with the surrounding decor also adhering to shades of red; whilst a feeling of reverent devotion in a person requires shades of blue for both.

Something similar holds good for the flow of time, in the dramatic action. If this goes over from the general interest one has at the beginning in character and action, to tragic catastrophe, this corresponds to a transition in the colouring from light yellowish-red, yellowish-green colours, to the greenish-blue and blue-violet colours. A progress of mood into cheerful pleasant comedy requires a transition from shades of green to yellowish-red, or reddish.

But that is only one stand-point. There is also another. This is that in the placing of the players, their characters are revealed in the colours they wear. One will not allow an angry person to appear in blue, but in a brightly-coloured costume, where one is dealing with a basically tragic mood. If the piece required it, however, one can allow an angry person to appear in a serious ceremonial blue, and it will then have a humorous effect.

If you put a joyously excited person against a blue background, and a miserable one against a yellow background you will give the impression that they are not in their right environment.

These subtle interchanges play between stage and audience.

An artistic, imaginative recognition of them belongs to the art of directing.

In the shading of light and colour of what appears simultaneously on the stage combined and harmonized with what relates to that which runs its course in time, the whole progress of the dramatic action from one aspect will be revealed. If this matter is grasped correctly, the objection cannot be raised that we are here advocating that the arts should be mixed up together in an inappropriate way. For in practice it will be found that the stage-director needs to find his way into colour quite differently from the painter. This depends on the fact that the painter allows his forms to be born out of the colour, whilst the art of the director allows character and action to radiate into the illuminated colouring of the scenery. A painter engaging in the latter becomes decorative in the bad sense; a stage-director indulging in the former kills the life on the stage.

In the case of a production in the open air, where one cannot reckon with the streaming of colour, one will need a much more colourful formation of speech and costuming which corresponds more clearly to the inner life of the characters than is necessary in the artificially constructed enclosed stage-set. That does not apply when nature is represented in a closed set. In that case, what has already been said in connection with colour-shading is absolutely valid.

We must strive in this way for stylization of light and colour on the stage. The stylization of the lines and forms of the plastic element however, would, on the contrary, appear artificial and mannered, a stylized forest, stylized architecture, have something of the nature of caricature, and in that case, a transition to a realistic representation will be necessary. Then that part of the drama which takes place in nature can be continued on the stage.

When right speech formation, through right gesture, within the right set is revealed, the spirit that lives in the drama will proclaim itself as soul from the stage and in such a proclamation only the artistic is possible.

Naturalism arises only out of impotence in face of artistic

forms. It arises when style has lost the spirit, and has degenerated into mannerism; but it will also, with the spirit, be found again.

CONCLUSION

In a remark we have included in the Foreword, Marie Steiner pointed out that the Speech and Drama Course was preceded by five classes on speech formation. This had not originally been intended, as the course should actually have begun on 2 September. However, Dr. Steiner's arrival was delayed. He had been travelling and still had a public lecture to give in London on 30 August. The return journey to Dornach had to be made via Stuttgart, where he was detained longer than he had intended by consultations, and a conference with the college of teachers at the Waldorf School on 3 September. This led to an introductory course in speech formation being given by Marie Steiner from 2 to 4 September for those waiting in Dornach. The actual Speech and Drama Course then began on 5 September and lasted until the 23rd. A good picture of these speech formation classes can be gained from a description Rudolf Steiner gave to the members of the Anthroposophical Society in the *Nachrichtenblatt*, of a similar speech course given in Breslau in June 1924. The crowd in Dornach in September was of course much larger, but since the description of the Breslau course is applicable to the Dornach occasion, we reproduce it here:

'So many applications were received for a course on the treatment of speech as an art, that the number of participants had to be restricted. It lies in the nature of such a course that those taking part should have the opportunity of actual practice in speaking, and for this reason it was not possible to have an unlimited number. On this occasion, though, a compromise was made. A possible number of participants was directed to the front rows, and they did the actual exercises, whilst the majority sat further back and absorbed what they could through listening silently. Frau Marie Steiner chose this method because she wanted to meet this overwhelming interest being widely shown in anthroposophical circles for the art of speech. This interest is gratifying to the highest degree, for it shows a growing understanding for that particular artistic treatment of speech, developed by Marie Steiner, out of the spirit of Anthroposophy. It can only be hoped that through a further growth in this understanding, this art of speech will gain access to ever wider circles. This could work really beneficially in view of the great significance this art has for cultivation of the personality.'

INDEX OF GERMAN EXERCISES

EXERCISES GIVEN BY RUDOLF STEINER

VERSES AND EXAMPLES BY RUDOLF STEINER AND OTHERS

INDEX OF ENGLISH EXERCISES

CHRONOLOGICAL TABLE

of courses, and other events in connection with the contents of
this book, given by Rudolf Steiner and Marie Steiner-von Sivers.

1919

Stuttgart: 26 August – 6 September	Rudolf Steiner: General Education Course. Speech Exercises in co-operation with Marie Steiner for the College of Teachers of the Waldorf School (before its opening).

1920

Dornach: 29 September 6 October 13 October	Rudolf Steiner and Marie Steiner: three meetings on the Art of Declamation arranged during the first course of the Hochschule at the Goetheanum.
Dornach: 4 October	Rudolf Steiner on Speech Disturbances in answer to a question at the Goetheanum.

1921

Dornach: 6 April	Rudolf Steiner on the Art of the Spoken Word, with examples of recitation by Marie Steiner.
Dornach: 10 April	Rudolf Steiner on Dramatic Art, in answer to a question.
Darmstadt: 30 July	Rudolf Steiner on Poetry and Recitation, with examples of recitation by Marie Steiner, during the Course 'Anthroposophy and Science' arranged by students of the College of Technology (25–30 July).
Dornach: 11–16 October	Rudolf Steiner: Orientation Course on Anthroposophy, the Threefold Social Order, and the Art of Lecturing, held at the Goetheanum.

1922

Vienna: 7 June	Rudolf Steiner on Poetry and Recitation, with examples of recitation by Marie Steiner, during the West–East Congress (1–12 June).
Dornach: 15 July – 5 August	Marie Steiner: Course on the Cultivation of Speech as an Art, at the Goetheanum, with explanations by Rudolf Steiner.
Stuttgart: 2–15 October	Marie Steiner: Course on the Cultivation of Speech as an Art, during the Youth Course, with explanations by Rudolf Steiner.

1923

Stuttgart: 29 March	Rudolf Steiner on Recitation and Declamation, with examples of recitation by Marie Steiner during the conference for Art and Education at the Waldorf School.
The Hague: 13–18 November	Marie Steiner: Course on the Cultivation of Speech as an Art, with explanations by Rudolf Steiner.

1924

Breslau: 7–16 June	Marie Steiner: Course on the Cultivation of Speech as an Art, during the Conference for Anthroposophy and Education.
Dornach: 2–4 September	Marie Steiner: Five lessons in a course for the cultivation of Speech as an Art, preceding the Speech and Drama Course.
Dornach: 5–23 September	Rudolf Steiner and Marie Steiner: Course on Speech and Drama given for the Section for Speech and Music at the Goetheanum.